PREACH WITH POWER:

A PRACTICAL GUIDE
TO CRAFTING
EXPOSITORY SERMONS
LIKE AN EXPERT

PREACH WITH POWER:
A PRACTICAL GUIDE TO CRAFTING EXPOSITORY SERMONS LIKE AN EXPERT

JOSÉ M. MORAL

Preach with Power: A Practical Guide to Crafting Expository Sermons Like an Expert

Library of Congress Control Number: 2022917251

ISBN:	Softcover	978-1-7332337-5-0
	eBook	978-1-7332337-6-7

Published by:
Full Editing

Email:
jmoralhdez@gmail.com

Web:
jmoralministries.org

Interior design:
José M. Moral

All scripture references are taken from the 1960 *Reina-Valera Bible* unless otherwise noted.

Second edition

Categories:
Religion, preaching, exegesis and homiletics.

DEDICATION

I dedicate this book to my dear readers
as sincere gratitude for choosing to read my books

and to those who wish to join in the difficult task
of preaching the Gospel of Christ.

ABOUT THE AUTHOR

The author has been a pastor for more than forty years. He served God as district director and administrator in different institutional areas. However, evangelism is one of the main fronts in which he participates, which credits him with a vast body of experience that he wants to share with those who aspire to perform successfully in the mission field.

Regarding his academic level, he is a seminary graduate with master's and doctorate degrees, the latter emphasizing church growth. This instruction has served him to find new congregations and collaborate in the development of the churches in which he has worked. Pastor José M. Moral currently works as an evangelist.

SYNOPSIS OF THE BOOK

Preach with Power: A Practical Guide to Crafting Expository Sermons Like an Expert is a self-help book. It is not just for beginners but also a guide for preachers who want to simplify the way they prepare their sermons. The book describes in four easy steps how evangelists can create their speeches in the shortest amount of time. This book does not tell you what to do; it teaches you how to do it.

It also explains some of the most pertinent aspects of Christian preaching: how to organize the biblical text with emphasis on the correct reading of the text, creation of the textual outline, identification of applicable terms for the sermon, and expository organization of the content. In addition, it shows the essential techniques of correct textual analysis, the three fundamental aspects of retouching the outline, and the importance of the personal documentation of the preacher.

The book is a guide that helps preachers to reach their goals easily. It takes the basic concepts of preaching and simply explains them. This book is a tool for preachers to grow in exegetical and homiletical knowledge of preaching. In short, the author's goal is to put theory into practice in the simplest way possible so that preachers write sermons with a professional level of organization and achieve the long-awaited goal of preaching with power. May God bless you in the most challenging undertaking: leading sinners to Christ.

THANKS

I appreciate you purchasing my books, which are valuable tools for preachers who want to improve their preaching techniques. Also, I appreciate your interest in sharing the Gospel of Jesus. I believe this book, *Preach with Power: A Practical Guide to Crafting Expository Sermons Like an Expert*, will walk you step-by-step through building the expository outline format most preachers would like to learn. It will also help you create your own homiletical and exegetical style.

If this self-help book is helpful to you, I thank you for recommending it to those who, like you, want to preach the Gospel of Christ. If you don't mind, maybe you can leave a comment on the sales platform where you bought it. This will help the book to have greater visibility and reach others more quickly.

I wish you much success for Christ.

José M. Moral

Índice

INTRODUCCIÓN

If you opened this book, it is because you are interested in the subject of evangelical preaching and want to preach your sermons with power. This is a guide for you to achieve it in the shortest time possible. This text practically puts the elements of professional preaching at your fingertips and makes the creation of the expository sermon a simple task and within everyone's reach. You can do it.

Preach with Power: A Practical Guide to Writing Expository Sermons Like an Expert focuses on two significant themes in preaching: biblical sermon preparation and individual preacher growth from experience. The above benefit is achieved by understanding and applying the three basic elements of expository preaching: the importance of exegesis, mastery of homiletical rules, and refinement of sermon exposition.

This is not a theoretical homiletics book focused on making specific rules known; it contains practical teachings that seek to show you step by step the most straightforward ways you can create an expository sermon that you then preach with power.

This text's objective is simple: Based on the experience of more than forty years as a preacher, I transmit helpful advice obtained during my years of study. It shows you that you don't need to take expensive academic programs to preach the sermons that many want to hear.

I share with you simple, practical rules that can make the difference between failure and success for a preacher. If you learn them and put yourself in God's hands, you will reach your goal in a short time. You will understand that anyone who wants to can preach well. Well, preaching is available to everyone because Jesus sent his followers to preach to the whole world (Matthew 28:16–20), and among those he sent is you, who now have this guide in your hands.

This book will guide you to become a powerful preacher. First, it shows the essential steps to help you craft a quality expository sermon. Next, it guides and helps you put together your sermon from the biblical text you prefer. Finally, it shows you the steps you must follow from when you choose the text until you finish your sermon.

This guide does not pretend to be exhaustive. Still, it explains four essential steps in constructing the biblical sermon: thematic organization, textual analysis, retouching of the document, and personal documentation. In addition, it exposes how you can prepare your sermon and contains outlines and templates that will serve as samples for you to make your materials and methods of homiletic and textual analysis.

The goal is that when you prepare your sermon,this manual will guide you until you manage to do it yourself. Then your perspective as a preacher will grow.

If you follow the steps outlined in this guide, you will easily preach from any Bible text you choose. Your listeners will enjoy it and be satisfied that you have grown a little more in your goal of becoming a powerful preacher. Before you study this book, you will notice a significant shift in your technical and spiritual understanding of homiletical and exegetical insights, which can help you powerfully preach—perhaps your most cherished spiritual goal during years of unsuccessful attempts. I wish you success in the company of preaching the gospel, and I ask God to guide you and accompany you in your purpose. I pray that you will achieve your goal of being a successful preacher. May God bless you a lot, and may you preach with divine power.

Thank you for purchasing this book.

The author

STEP 1

THEMATIC ORGANIZATION

One of the essential aspects of good preaching is the homiletical organization of the sermon. This is the first step to success in preaching. It said, "Order is the first law of heaven." It is the first law of everything that triumphs in life and even in nature, even in adverse natural events. For example, a hurricane would not be such if it did not achieve a high level of organization of the winds around a defined area of low atmospheric pressure. Therefore, homiletical rules ensure that the preacher establishes the necessary order in his sermon.

The word "homiletics" comes from the Greek *homiletics*, what reunion means, and *homileos*, which symbolizes converse, although it has a broader sense than its root: "from the Greek *homileus*, talking, to chat; i.e., a family conversation. Homiletics is a branch of theology that deals with the art and science of Christian preaching and the nature, classification, analysis, construction, and composition of a sermon" (Instituto Hispanoamericano de la Misión, 2018). The homiletical rules can help you compose a sermon you preach with power.

In a good sermon, the order of ideas stands out. When you select a passage that caught your attention, what you have is raw material. You have not created anything. You don't have a sermon. To preach with power, you have to create. Organize the ideas to the highest possible level. Don't settle for a few textual observations.

The sermon is an oratory piece that bears the imprint of the personality of the person who created it. It is unrepeatable. Other preachers can take your ideas, but not your speech, to make them their own. They would have to copy and read it as if it were their own; if they do it without your permission, it is plagiarism. It is a crime.

The secret to your success in expository preaching is organizing the text's content as much as possible. So may your sermon bear the stamp of your personality. The textual organization begins with four necessary exercises: critical reading, textual outline, identification of terms, and expository organization.

Critical reading

Read the text critically. Don't act on the latest opinion you hear or read. Develop your own criteria and make decisions for yourself. Regardless of whether it's good or bad, sponges absorb what they touch. They do not distinguish between what is useless and what is worthwhile. That can happen if you read the Bible or study different lexicons and biblical commentaries without considering the type of reading you do. The Bible does not contain immoral teachings, but the goal is to find what is relevant to your preaching and leave out what is irrelevant. That might be useful for another topic. You may absorb everything without realizing what information you got. You are not a sponge.

You can read to entertain, inform, learn, and investigate. When you read to consider, you excite emotions. If you read to inform yourself, you satisfy your curiosity about something, and if you learn, you acquire knowledge. But when you investigate, you expand the teachings you received. You grow more.

What is critical reading? Critical reading is different from other types of reading. It goes beyond remembering that you read one thing or another. It requires you to develop essential skills. The researcher not only memorizes content but deciphers the message behind the read text. Search the meaning within the text, known as reading between the lines. It is the message that most do not identify when they read. But you must achieve it because the preacher is a specialist who tries to show novelty to the audience. Therefore, you must learn how to read between the lines.

It is not enough for him to read and remember what he read. His interest is to find textual similarities and differences. It is complex work, but if you want to preach with power, you must cultivate a critical mindset. You must learn to identify the parts and separate them from the whole, isolate them and make them into a single piece of speech. Your sermon.

To achieve this, you need to read the same text many times. Read the passage as many times as you need until you understand it. Some experts advise that you read it about fifty times while thinking and reflecting on what you read. At the same time, write down the data you find and the ideas that come to you. It is a suitable method. As you read and analyze the reading, classify what you see and write down the details.

Relate in columns the material found when reading the text. Create categories. Distinguish between similar and different. Group the linguistic terms into families: similar words, thematically similar phrases, verbs, nouns, adjectives, questions, stories, characters, virtues, sins, curses, benefits, and any clues that point to the meaning of each textual detail. This is just an example, may be much more. It is a helpful exercise before writing the sermon outline.

Textual sketch

The outline of the text is the structural basis of the Christian oratory. It is the foundation from which the sermon's outline is born. The textual scheme is not the same as the sermon outline; the latter stems from the former. From the examination of the text, one or a series of summaries may emerge. Remember that the Bible is the Word of God, and this is an infinite source of wisdom. It's not like the other books.

You'll probably never outline a storybook or newspaper, but sketch what you read in the Bible if you want to preach well. First, learn the technique of sketching. Discovering the hidden pearls in the biblical text is a suitable method.

According to the Royal Spanish Academy (RAE), a sketch is "the first and not the definitive trace of a pictorial work, and in general of any intellectual or artistic creation. Vague or preliminary idea of something" (RAE, 2017). For the RAE, sketching is "arranging or working on something without finishing it. Vaguely indicate a concept or plan" (ibid.). First, outline the author's central idea. Next, the painter creates a pencil sketch. Finally, the preacher outlines the biblical text on natural or electronic paper.

The outline is the backbone that organizes the biblical material you discuss. The creation of the structure will serve as the basis for the birth of a new creature: your sermon. Concentrate on short sentences and the salient aspects of the text and then identify essential data and classify them. Preaching well, among other elements, involves knowing how to distinguish some truths from others and refer to a particular topic. In most cases, the audience does not understand too much content at once. Therefore, simplify the teaching and do not overwhelm the listeners; to achieve this, you must fully understand the meaning of the text.

It's hard for you to know the teachings of a text if you don't even know what the author said. That is why the outline of the text is necessary. The different levels of the scheme bring closer to the reader's view of the various themes focused on by the author of the biblical portion you study.

The work involves discovering the skeleton of the narration and the type of writing used, whether a poem, a psalm, a song, proverbs, or a story. First, you should know what the author said. When you investigate that, you get helpful information about the text. Then organize the material as best as possible to make it easier for you to understand the correct meaning of the topic you are researching.

After you choose a biblical portion and read it several times, it is the first job to outline the text. Look at the outline of the following text. Analyze the way to the Father Jesus announced to his disciples in (John 14:1–14).

I. Jesus's promise to his disciples (John 14:1–3)

- A. Jesus directed his disciples (v. 1).
  1. Do not trouble the heart (v. 1a).
  2. Belief in God (v. 1b)
  3. Believe in me (v. 1c)

- B. Jesus promised his followers (v. 2).
  1. The Father has many mansions (v. 2).
  2. I do not lie (v. 2a).
  3. I will prepare a place for each one (v. 2b).

- C. Jesus assured that he would leave and return (v. 3).
  1. He will come back for us (v. 3a).
  2. He will take us with him (v. 3b).
  3. We will live with him (v. 3c).

II. Jesus the way (John 14:4–6)

A. Jesus revealed what is necessary for our salvation (v. 4).

1. He suggested the origin of his abode (v. 4a).
2. He pointed the way to that abode (v. 4b).

B. Some do not understand Jesus (v. 5).

1. Ignorance of Thomas (v. 5a)
2. Thomas' insecurity (v. 5b)

C. Salvation is Jesus (v. 6).

1. The way is a person (v. 6a).
2. Truth is a person (v. 6b).
3. Life is in a person (v. 6c).
4. There is no other way apart from Jesus (v. 6d).

III. Relationship of Jesus with his Father (John. 14:7–11)

A. Clarification of Jesus (v. 7–9)

1. Human misunderstanding (v. 7)
2. They did not know Jesus (v. 7a).
3. They did not know the Father (v. 7b).
4. Divine likeness between Jesus and the Father (v. 7c)

B. Philip's insistence (v. 8)

1. He called Jesus Lord (v. 8a).
2. He asked to see the Father (v. 8b).
3. Conviction subject to evidence (v. 8c)

C. Questions of Jesus (v. 9)

1. Still don't know me? (v. 9a)
2. Why do you ask to see the Father? (v. 9b)

D. The works of Jesus (v. 10).

1. Unbelief prevents seeing the relationship between Jesus and the Father (v. 10).
2. The problem is doubt (v. 10a)
3. Jesus's words are the key to understanding where he came from (v. 10b).
4. Jesus does not act independently of the Father (v. 10c).
5. The Father acts with Jesus (v. 10d).
6. The works of Jesus belong to both (v. 10e).

E. Jesus's invitation (v. 11)

1. Believing in me is possible (v. 11a).
2. Jesus's works prove his provenance (v. 11b).

IV. Possibilities of the followers of Jesus (John 14:12–14).

A. He who believes in Jesus obtains his power (v. 12).

1. He will repeat his works by faith (v. 12a).
2. He will surpass Jesus in works (v. 12b).
3. Jesus supports the believer's faith in him (v. 12c).

B. He who asks in Jesus's name receives an answer from God (v. 13).

1. Ask the Father (v. 13a).
2. Ask in the name of Jesus (v. 13b).
3. Jesus will answer (v. 13c).
4. The goal is glorifying the Father (v. 13d).

C. The secret of the believer's success is Jesus (v. 14).

1. Ask in the name of Jesus (v. 14a).
2. Jesus will answer your request (v. 14b).

The correct outline does not take away or add to the text but relates a synthesis of the ideas in the passage.

A story or text outline is not a sermon. It is an outline of the teachings embedded in the story or content. You can reach it, but do not stay in the textual outline. Settling for that is like selling raw materials. You haven't built anything yet. Giving people bread is not the same as giving them a little wheat flour. They won't feel the same. The textual organization is just the beginning because before you create your own sermon, you need to understand what each verse and part of it is about. I do not deny that once this work is done, it can be tempting to stay put and go preach it.

Commodity sellers sometimes feel cheated by buyers. This is because the latter transform the raw material into products and multiply their profits by a higher percentage than the former. Sometimes, they even get rich in a short time. While the former work, sometimes more than they thought, they receive less profit than the buyers of their product because what people value most is creativity.

If you analyze the previous outline, you intuit that more than one sermon can come out of it. That depends on the approach and what you intend to teach people—as we will see later. For now, only the outline of the reading is of interest. You must learn to interpret what you read; what matters to the preacher is understanding the text's explicit or implicit message. Without an interpretive mind, it is difficult to go deeper. You do not develop critical thinking.

You can polish the reading that seems trivial to you, that you sketch with reluctance until it shines like a diamond. The sermon's outline or sermons derive from it because the text can become a series of speeches.

Then the sermon outline will come out of the text sketch you create first. It arises from hours of meditation. Analyze each phrase, word, and verb in the text, adjectives that define characteristics, nouns that act in the scene, and others found in the content. Identify the text particles and isolate them until they shine on their own. The stars are little gems lost in the vast interstellar space. But no one notices them until they are observed apart from the others.

Identification of terms

Another aspect to take into account is linguistic analysis. You chose a passage of Scripture, outlined it, and then broke it down into logical parts. Identify the sentences the text contains and classify each word of the expression you organized in the outline. Select the textual content. Choosing is distinguishing between the same or different and separating them into groups.

Reread the text several times; it doesn't matter if you go over fifty readings of the passage as you rip it apart and analyze every particle of it. Then reread the passage in light of the textual outline, no matter what you outlined. Finally, identify the main aspects and classify them on a piece of paper. It is the working method that yields the desired fruit for you.

The first time you classify textual content is the most difficult. However, learning how to do it is easy, and you will save time later. As the saying goes, time is money; manage it well to produce tangible benefits. If you correctly classify the material you find in the reading, the rest is perfecting the document. Pay attention to every textual detail, and you will better understand the thematic issue of the text.

The preacher is a scholar who knows what he reads. Philip asked the Ethiopian, "Do you understand what you read?" (Acts 8:30). Philip's question did not suggest that the eunuch did not know what he was reading. Still, he could help him understand the text of Isaiah. He was there to help him.

The preacher knows and conveys an appropriate message. Exhales confidence in the listener. Helps you understand. But that happens if you master the subject perfectly. Find out even the most insignificant details of the chosen text. Another key to biblical interpretation is understanding that those who wrote the Bible did not divide it into chapters and verses.

Writing contains many parts, books, chapters, paragraphs, sentences (phrases), and words, but the Bible also has verses. And this is one of the aspects that confuses some preachers because they do not distinguish the thematic approximation between verses.

The writers of the Bible wrote without dividing the text; they did not write chapters and verses as we know them today. Those divisions arose later to facilitate study, but today's divisions into chapters and verses sometimes make it difficult to understand the original message.

The average preacher frames his theme in the verses he chooses for his sermon. It's a job done; it seems easier to him, so the speaker starts from the verse as the vital particle of his presentation. This method can be helpful, but sometimes, it does not produce the best display results. It is known as the Probative Text Method.

The proof-text method is the most common preaching system among preachers, especially beginners. The first and sometimes only tool of many novice preachers is a Bible with a concordance. They think it is impossible to preach without it, but it is not valid. It is a valuable tool but not essential.

Your Bible concordance is limited, minimal in resources, and essential in content. Because complete Bible concordances are expensive, they relate the theme to all its verses from different thematic and alphabetical angles. It's easy to look up a word in the concordance and find several verses that mention it for various reasons. Sometimes, without noticing that detail, the preacher takes verses because of the similarity of certain words, without caring about the context, and includes them in the theme, and the sermon is done. They call it a thematic sermon, but this is nothing more than a chain of verses put together for a specific purpose. A Bible study.

It is not a sin to preach a topic. Sometimes, this may be the best way to teach a specific doctrine or demonstrate a particular issue. For example, Jesus preached a thematic sermon on the road to Emmaus: "And beginning with Moses and continuing through all the prophets, he declared to them in all the scriptures what they said about him" (Luke 24:27).

Jesus's theme was the earthly mission of the biblical Messiah. Walked Cleopas and his companion through the Bible from beginning to end. He taught them the meaning of the events that discouraged them. The study of Jesus was a masterful piece. The listeners recognized the power of Jesus's message: "And they said to one another, Did not our hearts burn within us, while he spoke to us on the road, and when he opened the scriptures to us?" (Luke 24:32). Thematic sermons are not wrong or forbidden, but the preacher can aspire to do more. The expository sermon is analytical, thus taking the preacher and the audience further.

It is difficult to preach topics for many years to the same congregation. Before long, the Bible appears to some preachers as a depleted source. When the speaker runs out of issues, he digs into a trodden field without new approaches emerging. He thinks he's already said it all. Some even ask to be transferred to another church. In the Bible, they have an infinite gold mine within reach. But still, they do not see the precious treasure they paw for without noticing it. Because they don't have the proper training.

Then textual analysis comes into play: exegesis and expository preaching from the text. It is how the Bible becomes an inexhaustible source for the preacher. As part of this textual interpretation, the analysis of linguistic terms is practical. That is why you should look for similarities and differences between the different parts of the text.

Selection of terms

Analyze the list of words and grammatical terms you created

from the first readings of the text. If you have not done so, isolate nouns, verbs, adjectives, blessings, sins, consequences, promises, and everything that catches your attention in the analyzed text. Under these words that head the lists, list what you find that concerns them. Create columns of like terms: two nouns, three verbs, two adjectives, three blessings, four sins, two consequences, one promise, and others. Include anything you find that catches your eye. Then polish the list. Refine it.

Thousands of species and different forms coexist in nature. There are biological, physical, and chemical differences and many other characteristics. Variety is everywhere. The same thing happens in the Bible. Diversity is the keynote of the universe. Art consists of the identification of similar and different elements. Take what interests you, separate it from the rest, polish it, and place it in a prominent place where those who see it will perceive the difference. That is the homiletical basis of a good sermon.

As in nature, words contain infinite possibilities. In addition, a literary text has syntactic and grammatical variety, and each difference in expression indicates a different meaning. Therefore, you must classify the textual content before preparing a sermon.

Observe the way an auto mechanic works. The different parts of an engine can be classified into containers: screws, nuts, washers, pins, pulleys, pistons, rings, and others. It is easy for him to report the content to the boss. The classification guarantees a logical order in pieces. For example, if he had to talk about screws to someone, he would organize them by measurements: an inch, a half, a quarter, an eighth, or by thread types—fine, medium, coarse, and other morphological details. Think of a mechanic who throws the parts into a big jar. The boss comes and asks for a report on them. You can't give it to him.

It is the same thing when you want to interpret a biblical text. You must classify the content before talking about it; you can't give an excellent biblical report if you don't classify and organize the text. You get the raw material for your sermon from the sketch you made of it. The different types of words you find are the pieces of your speech. Organize them as well as possible, and you will render a good report.

Grab your computer, then open Word or your favorite text program. If you don't use a computer, have a pencil and paper ready, and if your list isn't thorough yet, write down the relevant words and phrases in columns. The first classification identifies the essential expressions of the text outline. Then you classify the terms of each sentence. The list can be extensive; it will probably take you more than one page. Finally, select what you read and classify it with the corresponding Word. This homiletical exercise sharpens your imagination and helps you distinguish between words and phrases.

> When you learn to distinguish one element from another, you see it at first sight because you do it reflexively. Then, with practice, you condition your mind to textual analysis.

When you train, you look at the texts differently than you did before. You cultivate an exegetical mindset. When you learn this technique, you will never be the same preacher you were before. Practice will help you look at the text's content with the naked eye. I assure. Practice it, and you will see.

For example, nouns are the names of people or things. Under the word "nouns," create a column with the terms you found in the text: people, animals, or something. Then match the verbs in another column; they are the actions of the nouns. Likewise, classify the adjectives; they reflect the characteristics of nouns. Finally, find each species or family of words within the outline. You will find everything. It's fun. Please don't get tired. Classify them. This is the basis of expository preaching.

Don't worry; select the terms you find. It doesn't matter; put them where you find them when you need them. It is the raw material with which you will create sermons. This is a general grammatical classification of the text. You will see the particular details of each group of words or phrases. Classify everything you find.

Different types of classification exist; the main ones are grammatical and thematic. The first investigates the origin and meaning of words. Then the second is the relationship with the topic of the text. Both provide arguments that can guide you to different goals in the sermon. For example, sometimes, you preach the message of a specific word.

Do not exaggerate; identify each statement and catalog it with a word. That word will come in handy when you prepare your sermon outline. But of course, now it seems like a meaningless job to you. Still, you will see how the quality and quantity of your future preaching depend on this classification.

When you finish the classification, you will realize that single terms are not abundant. Meanwhile, other words or phrases appear more often in the text. A simple glance at the ranked list indicates the topics focused on by the author of the text. It is wonderful. Create your theme from the search for differences and similarities.

Definition of the topic

You may already feel like running to preach what you found, but now is not the time. You have only just begun the path to creating better sermons. The above classification suggests themes found in the text, but they are not sermons. Instead, each piece revolves around certain chosen elements: the characters involved, verbs used, qualifying adjectives, blessings granted, sins committed, consequences suffered, promises received, and all those themes that you have related during the study of the chosen text.

Each item can be a topic, but it is also likely to mean more than one. What you achieve will depend on how you observe and delve into the study. This is one of the ways to use the Bible as an inexhaustible source of knowledge.

Imagine that you found a person, a single noun. You think, what can I do with a character? You can create a biographical series. What you need is to delve into that person's behavior over time. Determine the distinctive characteristics of the individual: social origin, customs that formed his character, acquired defects, cultivated virtues, achievements, and everything you know about the subject. Each aspect of his character is a separate topic in a series about a character. The categories mentioned and those you find constitute the seed of future sermons. The thematic organization leads to the series of speeches. In one topic, you describe its failures, in another its virtues, and in the third, for what reasons it triumphed.

If you have three characters in the text instead of one, create a series that involves comparisons between different actors. In each theme, highlight their distinct characteristics and the differences and similarities of their temperaments, or create three series of other topics, one for each person found. The possibilities are limitless; even Balaam's mule, if you characterize it, can transmit a powerful message.

This method makes it possible to improve your preaching substantially. The topics found contain verbs used in the text. These adjectives personalize the subject, blessings promised or received, sins committed, consequences suffered, promises received, and more. Each classification announces a different topic for a sermon.

The secret is that you distinguish the textual content, even what the text says between the lines. The best sermons are not born from what is explicit but from what is implicit in the text. The obvious goes without saying. My Father used to say, "The grace of the barber is to leave a sideburn where there is no hair" because it is evident that what everyone sees does not have to be said. They already saw it, but the obvious leads to the hidden, what few perceive. Reading between the lines requires mental acuity.

For example, look at Jonah 1:5: "And the sailors were afraid, and each one cried out to his God; and they threw into the sea the belongings that were in the ship, to unload it from them. But Jonas had gone down into the boat and had gone to sleep." This text contains a message between the lines; the writing does not say so, but it is there. Perhaps that message is more important than what the text says about Jonah with his words that most people must have read many times.

Each sailor "cried out to his god." To what gods did they cry out? To idols. But the images do not answer anyone's prayers because they do not even know they themselves exist. Therefore, praying to the idols is meaningless, and many people know that. On the other hand, "Jonas slept," oblivious to the events. The only one with a real God slept instead of crying out to him for personal and collective salvation; worst of all, he was running from the only one who could save them. This is the message between the lines, but discovering it requires mental acuity. This is reading between the lines. The reason is what the narration suggests. Think about what you read and write from a correct interpretation of the text.

The most extraordinary richness of the text is between the lines. What could a story that happened so long ago and millions have read before you tell us if not? But reading between the lines requires you to read critically and exercise your mindset. It involves depth of analysis and mental acuity. Develop an analytical mind. Cultivate an exegetical attitude. An unknown text is not necessary for you to reach a new message. This is another of the mistakes of novice preachers: preaching from a strange text to say something that no one has heard, but they believe in it. They fail.

There is life in every text, verse, phrase, or word you read. Your job is to discover it. The worst strategy of a preacher is to choose an unknown text to say something new. What most shocks the audience is when you preach from a familiar verse and show its hidden face. As soon as you focus on the subject, the listener, who thought he knew everything about it, realizes his ignorance and does not miss a word of the sermon until you finish. Therefore, one of the essential aspects of explanation is clearly defining the topic of the text.

The subject is not the title; do not confuse it. The theme focuses on the general, the title on the particular—we will see it later. The topic is what your sermon will talk about: love, obedience, faith, kindness, and other pertinent issues. When you find the subject, you create the order of the sermon. Then you choose a keyword that identifies it.

The keyword

You can choose the keyword among those at the top of the list of words you created—the one you formed during the outline of the text. These words are the ones that give meaning and direction to the topic. They delimit it. They isolates it from the rest of the material you found. Identify the issues to be covered and place them prominently for your audience to see. Distinguish that part of the text from the pile of information located and indicate the details that you will present. The keyword exposes what you want your listeners to see and makes evident what is not seen with the naked eye. Indicate at once where you intend to lead the audience. Allow your sermon to turn toward a certain point: your objective.

In anatomy, it is said that we have a head, trunk, and extremities. Of that, there is no doubt. But we also have a neck. Imagine what it would be like to live without being able to turn your head from side to side. Even the robots look around. If we had no neck, we would live a miserable life. That is what happens to sermons that are born without a keyword. Rigidity makes those who deal with them unhappy.

The best keywords end in "S." Look at an example: your topic is love. You talk about love, quote biblical verses, and recount experiences of true love. Express personal concepts about love, get emotional, and cry if you remember what you have suffered for love. You laugh when you see yourself happy after the storm. Your listeners get excited about you. They cry and laugh at your tragedy mixed with blessings. They will say that it was a formidable sermon. I do not doubt it. It happens.

Someone will later ask, "What did the preacher talk about?" "Of love. I don't know. He talked about so many exciting things. They will say he made us cry and laugh like never before."

How many such sermons do you think you will preach without exhausting the theme of love? At this point, the keyword's value comes into play. Because it not only gives meaning and direction to the subject but also doses the presentation. See how it works.

Your theme is love. Greetings to the listeners. You give a short introduction about love, and at a certain point, you say, "Let's study some benefits of love." The keyword is "benefits." Your listeners know where you are taking them. This word rules out any argument that does not show listeners the *benefits* of love. It is not the only benefit. The word love frames an almost infinite territory of possibilities.

Love is not an emotion but a principle that can be absent or present everywhere and in any circumstance of life, even in the face of death. Love is the principle of God's universal government.

But with the same keyword, "benefits," you speak of the *benefits* of God's love, agape love; the benefits of love between brothers, filial love; and the *benefits* of conjugal love, Eros love. Thanks to the keyword, you have three different sermons on the same topic: love. It's not even all. The possibilities are limitless in any subject field. Therefore, each theme is like a tree full of branches in an infinite forest. If you change the keyword, you not only change the branch, but you can also change the tree.

What happens if you change the word *benefits* to *hexes*? Although you haven't changed trees yet, you can still stay on the theme of love. For example, you can say, "Let's analyze some *hexes* that lack of love brings to the family." However, with the word *hexes*, they can turn in another direction and jump to another topic—tree change. It's simple.

You can say, "Let's look at some *hexes* that sin brings to our lives." You left the subject of love; now the issue is sin. This is a technique that you can use in any type of sermon.

If your sermon is thematic, you choose a keyword, take the concordance, and select verses that declare different curses that sin brings on human beings. You can do the same when discussing *blessings*, *attributes*, *customs*, *sins*, and any other keywords you choose for your sermon. The possibilities are endless.

The expository sermon, the one that this book teaches, is different. The keyword does not come from a simple search in a Bible concordance but after the biblical examination. The textual analysis takes you into the inexhaustible depths of the text. There you find different topics, select them, classify them by words, interpret what they represent, and name them: verbs, nouns, adjectives, sins, blessings, curses, virtues, promises, and everything you find. You do it during the textual analysis, and when it is finished, you study the inventory of what you saw.

As we saw, the words at the top of the list govern the family of terms listed below them. They are plural words, occupy a specific place in the interpretation of the text, and work as a keyword.

You select similar words or phrases from the study and determine which keyword best defines them. Then you place it below it until you complete the group. The keyword is the tag that describes them from then on. In that group, this is the keyword denominating them in your sermon. For example, if you found three *sins*, the keyword *sins* are the label that denominates the *sins* that you write down under it. If you found four important *verbs* and want to preach about them, the keyword is *verbs.* The same with each related group during the study. A sermon must have a minimum of two points and a maximum of four; some allow up to five and more.

I like three points. Experience shows that more than three issues force you to be superficial. Few auditoriums allow you to preach for more than thirty-five or forty minutes. You can preach as long as you want, but you won't be congratulated. Three points are enough.

Three people rule the universe; Paul mentioned three heavens. Jesus rose on the third day. Cornelius sent three men to see Simon Peter. He could send a legion; however, he preferred to send three soldiers. The three are in the whole Bible. Nowadays, business people talk about the power of three; books have been written about it. Don't tire people out.

If you have a lot of material, dose it and don't give it away all at once because most likely they won't understand it. If you found six instead of three blessings, see if you can classify them into different areas. For example, you could talk about three blessings for the family. With the rest, create another theme: three blessings for the church, society, or yourself.

The keyword offers unlimited possibilities for sermon focus. Mastering this technique is vital to preaching with power and for people to remember the teachings more easily. This "keyword" is one of the fundamental elements of sermon preparation. First, determine the exact direction where you project the speech. Next, get listeners to identify the speaker's teachings. Without it, the sermon is a rant, sometimes meaningless.

You have chosen the biblical portion, read it many times, and identified the characters, words, and memorable phrases outlined in the text. You have analyzed every detail of the content: historical, grammatical, spiritual, and others. But you haven't finished yet. You still don't have a sermon.

The chosen text contains one or several sermons defined by the keywords that determine what you will speak to your congregation. One teacher said, "Don't give them more than three beans; people won't digest them." Most people don't assimilate more than two or three ideas at a time; they get fed up. Analyze John 14:1–3 and note the function of the keyword in the outline.

"(1) Do not let your heart be troubled; believe in God and me. (2) In my Father's house, there are many mansions; if it were not so, I would have told you; I am going to prepare a place for you. (3) And if I go and prepare a place for you, I will come again and take you to myself so that where I am, you may also be."

This text contains some *declarations* of Jesus:

A. "Do not let your hearts be troubled; believe in God, also believe in me" (v. 1).

B. "In my father's house, there are many mansions; if it were not, I would have told you; I am going to prepare a place for you" (v. 2).

C. "I will come again and take you to myself so that where I am you may also be" (v. 3).

> The keyword can be *declarations.* The term *declarations* establish the main points of the topic. So before you outline your sermon, you should know what you will be talking about to your listeners.

By the keyword, you know that you will communicate to them some *declarations* of Jesus. Still, according to the content of the text, they could be *promises, blessings, requests,* or other chosen words. The keyword indicates the meaning of the predication.

When you identify the keyword of the topic, you may think that you already have the sermon but do not believe it. We are just beginning to organize it. You have only identified the central phrase of the chosen text. Each sermon carries a keyword. It defines the major divisions of your sermon outline. Then you polish and restructure them. Examine the interpretive variants that arise when you change the keyword. The variations lead to the thematic series.

Serial preaching

Serial preaching depends very much on the choice of *keywords* and their application to the sermon. Think about the textual outline you made of John 14:1–14. Perhaps you think that now you can preach on this text, but don't do it; there is still a lot to do for the outline before it can be preached. The text's outline begins the creation of the sermon or sermons. Then you will analyze what you will do with that sketch. This is just the classification of the seed.

Keywords are the seeds from which sermons are born. Which ones you choose depends on how many sermons you will create. You could pick a keyword and make a speech from John 14:1–14, but you would barely mention the highlights of the text. Remember that you don't have much time to tell people what you want to express.

The outline of John 14:1–14 contains four essential sections: Jesus's promise (John 14:1–3), Jesus is the way (John 14:4–6), Jesus's relationship with his Father (John 14:7–11), and the possibilities of the followers of Jesus (John 14:12–14). So you can preach a sermon of these fourteen verses. The keyword could be: "aspects" essential to understanding the promise of the Lord. Example:

In John 14:1–14, Jesus pointed out four distinctive *aspects* of the believer's hope. These are his promise to save lost humanity, the way to return to the Father, the relationship of Jesus with his Father, and the possibilities that the followers of Jesus reach if they accept Jesus. The volume of information is a lot. You would hardly mention the main divisions and say something about the secondary divisions and a brief comment on them. Maybe it would work as an introduction to a series.

The four divisions mentioned would be the main ones. Bulky. The other sections would be subordinated to each other below these. The sermon would be long and tire the preacher and listeners. You better create a series of speeches. It has been said that a preacher matures as such when he can preach in series.

You should create a series on John 14:1–14. Study this possibility and see how it changes the meaning of the message you want to express to the congregation. Serial preaching produces better results than solitary sermons. The series creates an expectation in the listeners. Connect the audience with the preacher for the duration of the series. They enable a higher level of interpretive and theological depth. The audience learns more. A good series of themes builds suspense and tends to engage listeners in attendance—it's the favorite technique of film and television.

If you create a series of themes, it is necessary to reform the textual outline. Make each major division of the text you outlined a separate topic and subordinate minor divisions below it to main divisions. First, look at the meaning of the example passage.

The first sermon explains the *Promise of Jesus* (John 14:1–3), and the second presents the way to reach that promise, *Jesus is the way* (John 14:4–6). The third communicates the *Relationship of Jesus with his Father* (John 14:7–11), and the fourth lists the *Possibilities of Jesus's followers* (John 14:12–14). To make this idea work, choose a keyword for each section of the text outline and divide it into independent sermons within the theme of John 14:1–14. Remember that the keyword is the one that gives meaning to the topic you are focusing on because it facilitates the presentation and clarifies the message to the listeners.

In this case, the keyword is *warnings*. Still, it could be anything else that defines what you want to express to the audience. Choose the most accurate or the one that best suits your purpose. You must adapt the outline to the new term every time you change the keyword to another. The keyword agrees with the main divisions of the sermon. He announces them so that listeners can distinguish the thread of the discourse.

The sermon outlined in a series

At first glance, the outline of John 14:1–14 contains a lot of content for a sermon. Study each verse and choose keywords that lead to different turns within the contents. The example includes keywords, but they are not the only ones that can work. Each author prints the desired turn without losing the thread of the theme of Jesus cited by John. The keyword is like the rudder of the sermon, leading you to a specific point: the focus. That works as a neck between the head, the sermon's introduction, and its body. If you find those precise terms and keywords, you will create a series on the commission of Jesus to the disciples.

Remember that in the expository sermon, the divisions are born of the text. So based on this premise, the following outline suggests a series of four expository sermons built on John 14:1–14. But first, you must choose how you want to manage the text content.

Analyze the outline of John 14:1–14 expository, the book's focus, and study the following four outlines.

Sermon outline 1

I. Jesus's promise contains *realities* that his followers must understand (John 14:1–3).

A. Reality 1: Some *dangers* lie in wait for us (v. 1).
1. We can get flustered and miss the objective (v. 1a).
2. Our faith in God can be weakened (v. 1b).
3. Despising Jesus is fatal (v. 1c).

B. Reality 2: There are *reasons* to trust his Word (vs. 2–3).
1. The Father has a place for believers in him (v. 2).
2. Jesus does not lie (v. 2a).
3. He will prepare a place for us (v. 2b).

C. Reality 3: Jesus left *promises* we must remember (v. 3).
1. He will come back for us (v. 3a).
2. He will take us with him (v. 3b).

3. We will live with him (v. 3c).

Note how the primary level "A" (of grades A, B, C, and others) of the topics of the analyzed text became the sentence "I" of the first sermon of the series. Then the secondary levels with cardinal numbers that were in the primary outline (the one of all the investigated text) became introductory classes "A, B, and C." The sublevels a), b), and c) finally became the secondary levels (1, 2, 3, and others, if any).

With the change, you deepened the subject. This is an outline of John 14:1–3, from just the first part of the initial textual outline. It's not the only one you can create. It's a possibility. It all depends on your focus and the chosen keyword. We'll see another example later. Remember that the above is a sermon outline, not a sermon.

It is a skeleton you must dress with meat and skin to give it a body and turn it into a living being. Preachers who do not meditate on what they read risk showing their congregations ghosts: skulls or amorphous mass. Skeletons without meat or skin or piles of boneless meat. Boneless meat or vice versa. Both are corpses condemned to oblivion. They make people afraid.

The sermon is a living being that must coexist with those who listen to it. Therefore, listeners must remember it with satisfaction.

Next, analyze the outline of the second part of the analyzed text: John 14:4–6.

Sermon outline 2

II. Jesus made important *revelations* that show the authentic way to the Father (John 14:4–6).

A. He revealed his relationship with his Father (v. 4).

1. He showed the dwelling they prepared for us (v. 4a).
2. He described the path to that parental home (v. 4b).

B. It revealed the human misunderstanding of its origin and destiny (v. 5).

1. Thomas did not understand the divine origin of Jesus (v. 5a).
2. Ignorance endangers salvation (v. 5b).

C. He revealed that he is salvation (v. 6).

1. The way is a person (v. 6a).
2. Truth is a person (v. 6b).
3. Life is in a person (v. 6c).
4. Without Jesus, there is no reconciliation with the Father (v. 6d).

First, Jesus showed them human and divine *realities* that we must understand so as not to risk our salvation. He then revealed timely *truths* to them, revealing his true identity and purpose. The keyword is *revelations.* In addition, he clarified his divine origin because he wanted them to trust him without question.

A series of themes should lead from one plot to another without violence. It goes from the simple to the profound. Contains thematic progression and directional sense. Leads to a specific goal. It's like climbing a ladder; each rung leads higher.

Sermon outline 3

III. Jesus recounted *pieces of evidence* of his intimacy with the Father (John 14:7–11).

A. Evidence 1: Jesus pointed out to the disciples their ignorance of his likeness to the Father (v. 7–8).

1. Human misunderstanding (v. 7)
2. They did not know Jesus (v. 7a).
3. They did not know the Father (v. 7b).
4. They ignored Son's likeness to the Father (v. 7c).

B. Evidence 2: Philip's contradiction speaks for itself (v. 8).

1. He said: Lord, and did not understand who is Jesus (v. 8a).
2. Asked: Show the Father (v. 8b).
3. It is enough (v. 8c).

C. Evidence 4: Jesus's didactic questions and reasoning show that he and the Father are equal (v. 9).

1. Still don't know me? (v. 9a).
2. He who has seen me has seen him (v. 9b).
3. Why do you ask to see the Father? (v. 9b).

D. Evidence 4: Jesus claimed that his works are enough to believe in him and the Father (v. 10, 11).

1. Unbelief impedes our relationship with Jesus (v. 10).
2. The problem is doubt (v. 10a).
3. Analyze whether Jesus's words are human or divine (v. 10b).
5. Jesus does not act independently of the Father (v. 10b).
5. The Father acts with Jesus (v. 10c).
6. The works of Jesus belong to both (v. 10d).
7. Jesus invites us to accept his union with the Father (v. 11).
   a) Believing in Jesus is possible (v. 11a).
   b) His works demonstrate his origin from the Father (v. 11b).

It examines the ascending line of the theme of Jesus: human and divine realities that we must understand, revelations of his true identity, and evidence of his relationship with the Father. Accepting these statements of Jesus opens infinite possibilities for his followers.

Sermon outline 4

IV. *Possibilities* of the followers of Jesus (John 14:12–14).

A. Possibility 1: He who believes in Jesus obtains his power (v. 12).
1. He will repeat his works by faith (v. 12a).
2. He will surpass Jesus in works (v. 12b).
3. From heaven, Jesus will support believers' faith in him (v. 12c).

B. Possibility 2: Those who ask in his name will receive the Father's answer (v. 13).
1. Trust in the Father (v. 13a).
2. Accept the work of the Son (v. 13b).
3. Jesus will respond to those who accept divine unanimity (v. 13c).
4. The goal is glorifying the Father (v. 13d).

C. Possibility 3: They will find an answer in Jesus (v. 14).
1. Ask in the name of Jesus (v. 14a).
2. Jesus will answer your request (v. 14b).

Discuss possible variants of the first sermon you outlined. Next, you will talk about the *warnings* that Jesus gave his disciples in John 14:1–3).

Note: To better understand the example in the previous outlines, I included the key phrase at the beginning of the main divisions.

I now have the keyword *warnings* at the beginning of the first-level divisions, which is unnecessary. It is a custom that creates harmful stereotypes. Unnecessary redundancy. I included them as a didactic resource so that you understand how it works. In practice, it is not used to always write the keywords on the outline.

Analyze other possibilities of interpretation

I. Sermon 1: The promise of Jesus. The keyword is *warnings* (John 14:1–3).

  A. First warning: Some dangers threaten the believer (v. 1).
    1. We can be troubled and lose the kingdom (v. 1a).
    2. Faith in God can waver (v. 1b).
    3. To distrust him means to die (v. 1c).

  B. Second warning: Every faithful believer will have a heavenly home (v. 2).
    1. The Father has many mansions in his kingdom (v. 2a).
    2. Jesus does not lie (v. 2b).
    3. Each one will have the house of their dreams (v. 2c).

  C. Third warning: None of his followers will be abandoned (v. 3).
    1. He will come back for us (v. 3a).
    2. He will take us with him (v. 3b).
    3. We will live with him (v. 3c).

If you change the *warnings* keywords to *promises* keywords or other terms, you tilt the sermon in another direction. Replace "warnings" with *assertions* and see the result.

• You will talk about the statements that Jesus made to his disciples in John 14:1–3.

  A. Jesus affirmed that we can be troubled (v. 1).
    1. If we are troubled, we lose the kingdom (v. 1a).
    2. Faith in God can waver (v. 1b).

3. Faith in Jesus is essential (v. 1c).

B. Jesus affirmed that each follower would have a house in heaven (v. 2).

1. The Father has many mansions (v. 2a).

2. Jesus does not lie (v. 2b).

3. Each one will have the house of their dreams (v. 2c).

C. Jesus affirmed that he would not abandon his followers (v. 3).

1. He will come back for us (v. 3a).

2. He will take us with him (v. 3b).

3. We will live with him (v. 3c).

Then change "affirmations" to *promises* and note the direction of the main divisions of the sermon.

- You will talk about the *promises* Jesus made to his disciples in John 14:1–3.

A. If they stand firm, they will be rewarded (v. 1).

1. Do not be troubled (v. 1a).

2. Belief in God (v. 1b).

3. Trust in Me (v. 1c).

B. I will give each of you a new house (v. 2).

1. The Father has many mansions (v. 2a).

2. Jesus does not lie (v. 2b).

3. Prepare a place for each one (v. 2c).

C. I will return again (v. 3).

1. He will come back for us (v. 3a).

2. He will take us with him (v. 3b).

3. We will live with him (v. 3c).

The possibilities are endless. The more you study the sketch, the more details you find. Every time you change the keyword, your message spins in a different direction. Sometimes, it's minimal, but it leads the listeners to another point, to the new target you chose.

Preaching is a flight that transports the audience to the airport where the speaker wishes to take them. Still, the keyword is the rudder of the ship that takes travelers where you want to lead them. When you master this technique, the rest is easy. You can do the same exercise with the other three sketches in the series. Analyze the following variation about the other sermons in the outline.

II. Sermon two: Jesus is the way. You will talk about Jesus's *revelations* to his disciples in John 14:4–6.

A. Have confidence in me (v. 4).
1. Know my abode (v. 4a).
2. Learn the way to my home (v. 4b).

B. Some do not understand me (v. 5).
1. Some ignore where I come from (v. 5a).
2. Ignorance endangers the journey (v. 5b).

C. I am salvation (v. 6).
1. The way is a person (v. 6a).
2. Truth is a person (v. 6b).
3. Life is in a person (v. 6c).
4. Without me, there is no reconciliation with God (v. 6d).

Revelations keywords represent only one possibility among many. You can search for other "keywords" and print small twists to the sermon's meaning. Each keyword that you apply requires that you adopt the interpretation of the texts of the outline divisions to it. You must refine them until each phrase harmonizes perfectly with the proposed theme without distorting the meaning of the text. Harmony creates sounds that are pleasing to the ear.

In sermon three, you will discuss Jesus's *clarifications* to his disciples in John 14:7--9. The above sketch is in the first person as if Jesus himself were speaking to the audience. The next one is in the third person singular, but it could also be written in the first person. It's up to you. They are twists that qualify the preaching.

III. Analyze sermon three: the text records clarifications about the relationship of Jesus with his Father (John 14:7–11).

A. Doubts about Jesus are unfounded (v. 7–9).

1. Human misunderstanding (v. 7)
   a) They did not know Jesus (v. 7a).
   b) They did not know the Father (v. 7b).
   c) They did not perceive the divine likeness (v. 7c).
2. Philip's contradiction (v. 8)
   a) He called Jesus, Lord, which means "Kurios, supremacy, supreme in authority" (e-Sword-the Sword of de Lord with an electronic edge. Version 3.0.0, 2000-2021). Lord is an attribute of God, and Philip did not perceive it (v. 8a).
   b) He did not perceive the relationship between Jesus and the Father (v. 8b).
   c) The presence of Jesus was not enough for him (v. 8c).
3. Questions of Jesus (v. 9)
   a) Do you still not know me? (v. 9a).
   b) Why do you ask to see the Father? (v. 9b).

B. The works of Jesus come from the Father (v. 10, 11).

1. Unbelief prevents a right relationship with Jesus (v. 10).
   a) Doubt kills faith (v. 10a).
   b) Jesus's words are not human (v. 10b).
   c) Jesus does not act independently of the Father (v. 10c).
   d) The Father acts in Jesus (v. 10d).
   e) The works of Jesus belong to both (v. 10e).

2. Two ways to believe in Jesus (v. 11).
    a) Trust the words of Jesus (v. 11a).
    b) Believe in the works of Jesus (v. 11b).

> Observe how the divisions of the outline adapt to the focus of the topic. The adaptation respects the text but includes keywords that identify a precise interpretation of the sense that the preacher emphasizes in the sermon. Remember, the teaching is in the text, and you organize it. You don't invent what doesn't exist. Your task is to discover and manage.

Do not transcribe the outline of the text; interpret the teachings implicit in it and create your own resume. Do not walk away from the explicit; read between the lines and discover the unspoken. One teacher said, "Don't hammer it in." The fit should be smooth. The force is out of tune.

The outline you made of the text is the basis for the various sketches in the series you intend to create. The textual organization is integral to the biblical text. Still, the creativity is in your ability to put little twists on the individual outlines. You create from the small thematic portions drawn from the textual outline. You developed it during the study.

> Each sermon outline occupies a fraction of the base outline but is organized and polished to the highest possible level. Herein lies the art of laying the proper foundation for powerful biblical preaching.

IV. Sermon 4: *Possibilities* of the followers of Jesus. You will talk about Jesus's *promises* in John 14:12–14 to those who recognize his divinity.

A. He who believes in Jesus obtains his power (v. 12).
   1. He will repeat his works by faith (v. 12a).
   2. He will surpass Jesus in works (v. 12b).
   3. From heaven, Jesus will support the believer's faith in him (v. 12c).

B. If you ask in Jesus's name, you will get an answer (v. 13).
   1. Ask the Father (v. 13a).
   2. Ask in the name of Jesus (v. 13b).
   3. Jesus will answer (v. 13c).
   4. The power of Jesus in his followers glorifies the Father (v. 13d).

C. Jesus guaranteed the answer to your requests (v. 14).
   1. Ask in the name of Jesus (v. 14a).
   2. Jesus will answer your request (v. 14b).

Maybe you think these outlines are ready to preach. But unfortunately, it is not true; they are nothing more than an outline of what your sermon will be. They are ovules, developing embryos.

Presenting this to people is like taking a fetus and saying: I present to you, my Son. They still need to mature and feed before they can exist. A set of ingenious ideas does not constitute a sermon. Each creature must develop until it shines with its own light. The sermon outline traces the route the preacher will take before the audience. It is the structure that supports the body of the sermon.

Expository organization

This is the part that some preachers are most interested in. The novice expositor prefers to create his sermon in a "jiffy"—as the saying goes, in an instant. We live in a time of express things: express services, kitchen to the minute, instant drinks, etc. The speed changed the way of measuring the distances between one point and another; time was reduced from years to months and weeks, and travel days to hours, minutes, and seconds. When you travel, the GPS converts the miles or kilometers to hours, minutes, and seconds. So speed affects our behavior.

The speed of our time dilutes life in a brief time. The transience of life and the urgency with which we live impose an environment conducive to bungling, carelessness, and emptiness. A Christian writer said, "Nothing great has been achieved without sacrifice."

The easiest thing for the preacher is to stand behind the pulpit. Open the Bible, read a text, close the Word of God, put it on the pulpit, and talk endlessly about what comes into his mouth. Again, preaching without order and, sometimes, even without content. The Spirit can use it. It is indisputable. But if you prepare yourself, it will use you better.

It is said that a good preacher presents to the audience ten percent of what he knows about the subject of his preaching. The preacher does not speak of imagination. It does not flutter like a frightened bird over any point. In the exposition of the sermon, there is a logical order and common sense. They say, "Common sense is the least common of the senses."

The sermon is like a living being born, growing and developing. It has vital parts like any living body. So before you create your first outline, you need to understand the sections of a sermon. The sermon outline delineates the fundamental parts of that new being that you will bring into existence.

Sermon divisions

As you know, the keyword determines the main divisions of your sermon. When you selected the keyword from each group of chosen words, facts, events, and others, you knew how many sermons your text contained. Rarely does a speech come out of the textual analysis. They are almost always multiple births. You open the page, electronic or physical, and arm the divisions of your sermon.

One of the benefits of this epoch is that you can save a lot of time. We will talk about technology later. Have an electronic template for my sermons. I will show it to you in this section.

You found three *declarations* of Jesus. So you extract the main idea of each declaration and write three short sentences. They are the three main divisions of your sermon.

• Go back to John 14:1–3.

A. "Do not let your hearts be troubled" (v. 1).

B. "In my father's house are many mansions" (v. 2).

C. "I will come again" (v. 3).

There you have the three *declarations* of Jesus in John 14:1–3. Nobody doubts that he said that, but those statements have complimentary phrases. Those other phrases can be the secondary divisions of your sermon.

• Write Jesus's *declarations* under each significant division. Example:

A. "Do not let your hearts be troubled; believe in God, also believe in me" (v. 1).
   1. It is good that they have faith in God (v. 1a).
   2. Trust me also (v 1b).

B. "In my father's house are many mansions" (v. 2).
   1. This is true (v. 2a).
   2. I do not tell lies (v. 2b).
   3. I will prepare a place for you (v. 2c).

C. "I will come again and take you to myself so that where I am you may also be" (v. 3).
   1. I will take them with me (v. 3a).

2. We will live together (v. 3b).

You can write them in the grammatical tense and person that you like to speak to the listeners. Past, present, or future; first, second, or third person; singular or plural—each one nuance as he sees fit. What is essential is the text's message to the preacher and how he conveys it to the listeners.

John 14:1–3 is the favorite passage of millions of Christians. Since Jesus promised these blessings, this promise has inspired thousands of preachers. I know I discouraged Christians who believe in God but lack faith. Jesus asks them: Belief in me; you have seen me. I will not fail you. You can tell everyone or one in particular. So say it. Don't shut up this good news.

Many people who repeat these verses from memory do not understand the perspective of this promise. Jesus promised his followers that he would fulfill their dream of having a house. Many people die on this earth without having a home of their own. They could never have it. They spent their money to live in someone else's house. Think of the thrill of owning a new abode—a unique home next to God.

He promised: I would take them with me, and they would be by my side. I will share my property with you. I will never abandon them. Will go back to where they should never have left. I will reinstate them to eternity.

You need to gather specific data and organize them to understand them in front of the audience. The order is necessary for there to be clarity in the ideas.

It is said that a particular novice preacher learned his sermon by heart. He went over it to exhaustion. Then, on the appointed day, he went to the temple. He climbed onto the dais, stood behind the pulpit, and greeted the audience with a smile on his lips. The brothers said: "Amen."

An ominous cloud suddenly enveloped the preacher. His face paled with fear. With the face of a corpse, he said, "John says, John says, John says, John says, John says, John." Until "What does John say?" interrupted a mocking listener. "One thing is John above and another John below," he said.

If you organize the sermon, you will avoid undesirable forgetfulness. Fears will disappear because your convictions will increase your confidence that the Holy Spirit is with you. Take a look at the following template for creating expository sermons. You can make the same or similar one, with blank spaces to fill in when preparing your speech. A guiding pattern is essential to maintain a standard order in your homiletic organization. It is the way your sermons can be organized in the same way. I will show you a copy of the one I use, but you can make your own.

Create a template for your sketches

Take a blank sheet of paper and write the title of the sermon. It is the first thing you do after you finish the textual analysis. Two inches from the top margin, center the following sentence:

Sermon title

Then leave two blank spaces and write the main data of the outline; they are the identification of your sermon. Do it as below:

Series: (Title of the series if it is a series)

Text: (The base text of your sermon)

Biblical reading: (The best verse or portion of the text analyzed in the textual exam. Beware, do not choose texts that are not related to the topic.) I always prefer a verse or portion that is key in the said sermon.

Hymns: (The hymns or songs that you will use in the presentation that announce the text's message or call to obey it. That reinforces the message).

> The above is data that you should have on hand. The first thing is the title of the series. Then, below, aligned to the left, is the descriptive data of the series (if it is a series) and the topic to be treated (if it is a single sermon, do not include a series).

Listeners are likely to ask you for the sermon or parts of it. Those who organize the cult or someone interested in your topic may want to get your arguments. Keeping the essential details of your issue close at hand suggests order. The organization is reflected in what you do.

The above heading follows the sermon's introduction with its main parts. I like to organize the outline with Roman numerals, uppercase letters, cardinal numbers, and small letters with parentheses. As it appears in the outlines in this book, it is known as the Harvard style. There are other styles, it depends on the taste of each one. The main thing is the clarity of the written message that will then be your guide in preaching in front of the audience.

I. Introduction

A. (Greetings)

B. (Brief explanation of the topic you will deal with)

C. (Transitional sentence with the keyword)

> The introduction is the head of the sermon; it creates a point that differentiates it from the other parts. It must be noticed with the naked eye.

Use specific numbers and letters for each section of the outline. Don't alternate them. Choose a format for each part and make it a permanent look. Using Roman numerals to distinguish level one, always use them in each sketch. If you use capital letters in primary sections, do not change them in another sermon to Roman numerals. You will end up confused. Uniformity is part of the order. Establish your own system. A good preacher is a system builder. It's coherent.

The introduction has three main parts: greeting the audience, a synthetic presentation of the topic you will present, and transitional prayer. The transitional sentence revolves around the keyword. It is the neck of the sermon. It is between the head and the body of the sermon outline, which follows the introduction. Look at the body example:

II. Sermon title

- A. (First division of the first level)
  1. (First secondary division)
  2. (Second secondary division)
  3. (Third secondary division) If there are more than two, include the ones you have. Remember that more than three or four is not convenient. There are exceptions.
- B. (Second division of the first level)
  1. (First secondary division)
  2. (Second to secondary division)
- C. (Third division of the first level)
  1. (First secondary division)
  2. (Second secondary division)

In Roman number two, write the title of the sermon. Then, under it, organize the primary, secondary, and other divisions, if any.

There you put the annotations and additional information you are afraid of forgetting.

> Do not overload it; if you overstock the annotation scheme, it ceases to be an outline. Instead, each paragraph must contain the topic essential that you will develop later.

The body of the outline is followed by the conclusion, which has several vital parts that play different roles during the exposition: didactic, persuasive, action, and spiritual.

III. Conclusion

A. (Recapitulation – A synthesis of the main points covered in the body, nothing more)

1. Summary of point one
2. Summary of point two
3. Summary of point three

B. Called

1. Persuasion to accept the exposed message
2. Commitment to God

C. Closing prayer or blessing (Put the audience before God so that the Holy Spirit can do its work).

After the conclusion, you include an aside to help your memory:

1. **Next title:** (Announce the next theme if it is a series. Sometimes, there are people in charge of announcing, but I prefer to do it. It is a hook that ensures the return of the listeners. Get to the point and do not beat around the bush. Be concrete and personable; you're the best person to invite listeners back.)
2. **Preached in:** (Below, you write down in numerical order the places where you preached that sermon.)

The conclusion, like the introduction, has three main parts: recapitulation, appeal, and closing prayer or blessing. Blessing the congregation is a method that sometimes substitutes the closing prayer. Instead of praying to dismiss the audience, some preachers consider it more appropriate at the end of the sermon to bless the congregation. They assume that enough has been prayed before. Also, sometimes you make an appeal and pray for the listeners. Then you don't want to sound routine, so you repeat or read a blessing and say goodbye. The Bible has many blessings. For example, some are 1 Corinthians 16:23–24; 2 Corinthians 13:14; Galatians 6:18; and Ephesians 6:23–24.

Search the Bible and keep a list of biblical blessings. Innovate. Be original.

Below you announce the following topic (if it is a series) and then leave a section for annotations; this last, in case you preach the sermon in more than one place. Sometimes, I even write down the names and dates that people from other sites were present when I preached the topic. It is not good to repeat. Smells careless.

Analyze the previous template and create one that will serve you to prepare your sermons. Then the main work is done. You repeat it whenever you want. That's what you need when creating a speech. Your job is to fill it with the new data, and that's it.

Analyze the template and determine where you are in creating the sermon. First, choose the theme, the biblical text, and perhaps the verses for the biblical reading, but the hymns you will use when expounding your theme you look for when you finish the outline work. Next, choose the keyword and create the main divisions of the sermon. Finally, you almost have the sketch of your speech!

The secondary divisions clarify the theme of the main divisions. They are included when you find a colon or more in the text.

Don't try to invent divisions if there aren't any. There may be many, but if there are several, it would be better to create another topic.

I had a sermon that, when I preached it, I was half done. I never had enough time. So I broke it down further and turned it into a series of eight sermons. So now I will talk about that topic for a week.

You do not have to fill out the entire template. If you have less material, remove the remaining points on the form. If you have a lot of arguments, add other paragraphs. More than two levels can be tricky. So many ideas together make your sermon complex; information-laden expositions tire listeners.

So far, you have achieved a good step. You have the sermon's topic, text, Scripture reading, keywords, and primary and minor divisions. Finally, you can think of the title of the sketch.

When a child is about to be born, the future parents think of names. Although the definitive name is given when the child is born, the birth of a new being requires a name. Similarly, if you think of a title, it helps you move in a specific direction.

Choice of title

When you choose the theme, you can write some titles. This is because many preachers prefer to headline last after the sermon. After all, sometimes, the course varies during the sketch's composition.

Even so, I prefer to put a title that serves as a guide, then I fix it, adapt it, change it, or polish it.

I don't like to act like those parents who will have a child and don't know what to name him or her when he or she is born. The girl or boy is born, and the legal officer comes to register him or her, and nobody knows what to call him or her. Sometimes, the innocent creature gets hurt with an unpronounceable name.

The headline is an art. It is not easy to create attractive titles. It is a skill that is studied separately. But don't worry too much about perfection; give your sermon a title. Most likely, you will later improve it, polish it, or change it. The important thing is that you stay on track when choosing the topic. Don't work randomly.

Years ago, I visited a carpenter in his woodworking shop. He built double beds. The furniture he made had mismatches in the joints. They lacked squareness in the corners, the wood was rough, and the drawers danced on the slides and frames. It didn't work well. I asked him, "How much do these beds cost?" "Depends on how they look," he said.

He didn't sell many and had to go to another job. Good architects include in the plans even the color of the building's final paint, the decorations they will put on the structure, and even the ornamental plants in the garden. Build well from the start. Lay solid foundations for your sermon. Improvisation leads to carelessness. Do not fool yourself. Most improvisers do not do such a feat; they can quickly organize the knowledge they have acquired over time. Nobody can give what they don't have. With practice, you too will develop many skills.

You analyzed the text and chose keywords, specific phrases, good or bad characters, and more. You identified the topic and created a title or several. You have hardly started the work, but the main thing is missing: keeping a record and polishing the achieved product. Document the sermon outline. You made reasonable arrangements and organized the material well, but it was not enough. You must apply correct textual explanation to the text. Exegesis will confirm your homiletical views.

STEP 2

TEXTUAL ANALYSIS

The second step is textual analysis. An explanation of the biblical text is the kind of professional search preachers of the Word use. The correct biblical exegesis has a series of steps you must learn.

> The exegesis contributes to answering some key research questions: what, who, to whom, how, when, where, and why.

Some preachers analyze the text before creating the outline, but that's not a good idea. Beginners surround themselves with Bible commentaries, Bible concordances, Bible dictionaries, and all kinds of tools that contain textual information. They spend hours lost in a jungle of knowledge; it is so much that the Muse gets entangled and does not arrive. Not the best technique.

With this method, when you get an idea, it is nothing more than repeating what others said. The originality disappears, so you will never be a father. That is why you did the work of the first step without looking at any other book than the Bible because you need to cultivate your ideas.

With step number two, you study the outline from the perspective of textual analysis. It is the verification of what you did in step 1.

Don't just analyze the text you chose for your sermon. Submit the selected text, the entire chapter, and, if necessary, the book to a full or partial textual exegesis. You need to understand the details of the text you chose and sketched.

Imagine a traveler who finds a coin on the road, looks at it, and says, "I must first check the surroundings to see if I should take it." He doesn't act like that. First, he takes it and then investigates what is necessary. If it has to be returned, he returns it; if not, it stays with him.

> Step 2 is the around-the-text review you chose. It is the one that allows you to know the details of the text. Reversing the steps can lead you to miss the target.

They say that a hunter bought a puppy of a kind of dog famous for its talent for hunting. He acquired it because he wanted to be more efficient in the hunts he went on with his friends. To achieve the goal, he gave special attention to the animal.

He fed it carefully and trained it to the maximum for months. The cub grew up and became a beautiful hunting animal. In a short time, he walked like a champion. The musculature of the dog heralded gains. The dog's owner's friends congratulated him on the purchase. When the hunter believed the animal was ready to produce profits, he took it to the bush to hunt.

As soon as they reached the hunting area, the dog saw a deer and ran after it. "Today, I will eat venison; I knew this dog was good," he thought.

The dog seemed to catch up with the deer, but a hare crossed the road, and the dog left the deer and ran after the hare. "Don't will eat venison, but the hare is not a bad option," the man thought. Then right away, a rabbit crossed in front of the dog, and the dog followed it. He thought the rabbit could also become as good a dish as a hare.

The animal suffocated, with its tongue hanging out of its mouth and barking like never before, and grazed the rabbit's tail at full speed with its sharp teeth. But a little mouse got between them. So the dog left the rabbit, ran after the little mouse, and finished the hunt by digging a hole under a dry tree in the forest. He couldn't even catch a mouse.

Something similar happens to those who reverse steps one and two in sermon outline preparation. Some get dizzy in the woods and don't see the details. "Don't trade a hare for a cat," as the saying suggests. Instead, please stick to the chosen text and document its content.

The textual explanation "is not pure research (Vyhmeister, 2009)." Still, it teaches you enough to learn what you need to know about the passages chosen for your sermon. Don't preach what you don't know. Your power as a preacher multiplies when your conviction of what you say grows. Doubt breeds fear. Ignorance attracts ridicule. Knowledge gives security and strength, but true power springs when human unites with the divine.

The preacher's true power arises when the human being joins the divine power. That relationship reaches a supreme level of collaboration when human knowledge unites with divine illumination through the Holy Spirit. So first, become a teacher of the Word; many will want to hear you. Then you preach with power because a force of divine origin is within your reach.

Perform the exegesis with investigative rigor. Carefully reread the text as many times as necessary, write down the details suggested by the analysis, organize the notes, and write the final document. Be precise. There is more than one type of biblical exegesis, but here we propose the order suggested by Professor Vyhmeister (Vyhmeister,

2009). A sound explanation, according to her, takes into account at least seven points.

Ask yourself the following questions and answer them with your explanation: (1) What is the canonical context of the text? (2) What does the original text say? (3) What message does the text contain? (4) What meaning does that message have? (5) Where, in what place and time, did the author and recipient live, and what was their historical, geographical, political, and cultural environment? (6) How did they understand the text's message? And (7) what does the text tell you today? The latter, in short, is what you most need to know.

Analysis of the canonical context

Canonical comes from canon. According to the RAE, the word "canon," among other meanings, means "rule or precept, catalog or list, catalog of books held by the Catholic Church or another religious confession as authentically sacred" (Española, 2014). In this case, the Bible is the canon that contains the sixty-six books that we consider sacred. However, the Catholic Bible includes apocryphal books.

Preaching with power requires that you know what you say. You begin your study with the canonical context, the context in which the book or part of it you are studying. It is the most exhaustive work. Go from the whole to the selected text. Investigate the context in which the book you analyze came.

Apocryphon means "False or feigned. Of doubtful authenticity as to content or attribution. Said of a book of the Bible is not accepted in the canon biblical such as the apocryphal gospels" (Española, 2014).

Use the legitimate biblical canon in your explanation. Analyze the book before researching the text. The book is the context to which the text belongs. Study the theme of the book. The reasons why the author wrote it. The date. Who ruled at that time? What were the political, social, cultural, and religious circumstances?

To whom he directed it. Find out all the details that interest you about that context. Become an expert on that book. Go from the general to the particular. Do not talk about the specifics before understanding the general. It is like studying a flower without knowing what plant was born. You are ready to research the text when you understand the author's purpose and the book's details.

As you know, the prophets wrote their books without the divisions that they have now. So they did not divide them into chapters and verses. But notice how sometimes these divisions seem to interrupt specific biblical themes. It is because the divide is not exact.

Preachers search the biblical text for entire portions of a topic. These portions are called "pericopes." A pericope is a piece that contains a complete message from start to finish. Before her and after her, the subject is different. Learning to distinguish one pericope from another is another of the secrets of creating good sermons.

It frames the content of a theme, scene, story, prophecy, parable, sermon, or any other delimitation established by the book's author. Some pericopes start in one chapter and end in the next. That suggests that you should delimit the thematic content to find a better approximation to the topic. Your text must include the analysis of the complete pericope. Examine your scheme.

Notice how the text is part of the canon. For example, the portion may contain one or more verses. Next, define the pericope in which the verses you chose. Then look at how it is involved in the rest of the book. Finally, check where its limits are.

The limits seem invisible, but they are there. A change of scene in the narrative, a different theme, a separate prophecy, or any other variation suggests the end of one pericope and the beginning of another.

Do not mix one topic with another that has nothing to do with it. Delimit each theme. Practice will help you choose well from the choice of text.

You can speak well without being faithful to the subject, but the sermon wanders. It is not concrete. My father, as an example of infidelity to the topic, recited a verse that someone wrote. It said,

Female, the cow, gave birth.
The night is over.
The archbishop died.
Eaten the roast suckling pig.

In Spanish, the four lines rhyme but deal with independent themes that have nothing in common. Focus on a specific topic. The rest is called inconsistency. Don't get sidetracked; stay on topic.

Exegesis allows you to find the correct meaning of the biblical interpretation. If you included elements from another pericope in the scheme, you could delete them or leave them. Assess what suits the sermon best.

Look for a Bible with notes in the margin. First, read some Bible introductions written at the beginning of each book. Or even consult a volume of comments on this. Then find out the context of the book.

Be careful when reading notes. Sometimes, comments reflect the influence of the author's theological worldview. For example, Paul wrote, "Examine everything; hold fast what is good" (1 Thessalonians 5:21).

Look at what others said about the text but be critical. Carefully examining geographical aspects, historical data, social characteristics, and others may be acceptable to any doctrinal position. Still, the author's theological presuppositions sometimes affect his interpretation of the subject. Choose the most respected authors. Consult several authors and discriminate in favor of the most exact.

Today, these tools are Bible commentaries. Bible dictionaries, Bible concordances, lexicons of original Bible languages, introductions to the books, interlinear versions of the Bible, and others. Moreover, these are more affordable than years ago.

Good theological dictionaries, Bible commentaries, Bible concordances, and others appear on the net. Again, there are free and paid. For example, e-Swords is one of the more complete applications for biblical research. This application, with the bibles and the elementary material it brings, is free. Still, you must buy the rest of the volumes. You can collect up to eighty documents, including bibles, commentaries, references, and dictionaries.

The application contains bibles in original and interlinear languages. Other programs such as Libronix and Bibleworks are also available online. Any of them contains the tools you need. It's incredible how much is available to you today. In addition, paid e-books are minimal in cost compared to paper volumes.

The funny thing is that, sometimes, we want to preach well without investing in tools. Ask a carpenter or any other worker if he can do it right without investing in tools. Invest and you will grow.

Almost anyone has access to these biblical research tools. But not everyone learns to use them. The paper book is easier to handle for most. But no matter what system you choose, study and you will get a clear idea of the canonical context you are interested in knowing.

Study of the original text

Get as close as possible to the original text. The best tools to achieve this goal are in original languages. Don't base your study on your favorite version of the Bible. Some versions are more accurate than others; there are even paraphrases of the Bible.

A paraphrase is a comment on the original text. It is not strict. Your explanation of the text must withstand textual criticism. Remember, you will make it public, and the listeners will judge it.

There are differences between one version and another. For example, there are popular and studio versions. A popular version is not the most appropriate to establish profound concepts of a biblical theme; the study versions are more reliable. If you don't know the original languages, it doesn't matter. There are interlinear bibles that you can consult. Find an interlinear of your tongue.

Among the best versions are Reina-Valera versions 1960 and 1995; Jerusalem Bible 1967; Latin American Bible; Lockman Foundation 1986; New Spanish Bible by Luis Alfonso Schokel; and Mateo Iglesias 1976. In English: New American Standard Bible and New Revised Standard Bible (Vyhmeister, 2009).

Consult them and find out if your chosen text contains textual variants. Text variants are small letter changes, added or omitted words, and repetitions. They do not affect the biblical message, but they can induce different points of view about it (Vyhmeister, 2009).

Determine what the original is most likely saying and compare it to your interpretation. Establish the textual evidence.

Understanding the text message

Since you figured out the canonical context and checked the textual evidence, you can interpret the text's message. To preach, use your Bible, a translation, but consult the original text first. Then clarify the announcement of the text.

If you want to preach with power, it is good that you acquire some valuable tools for the preacher. You don't have to invest a fortune. Just get some that are reliable.

Get a good Bible dictionary. A serious grammar of the languages of the Bible, Hebrew or Greek, depending on whether you study the Old or New Testament. A Bible as faithful as possible to the original languages, if possible—an interlinear version. The benefits you will get from them will be worth the investment.

The biblical dictionaries and grammar of the original languages establish the correct translations of the text. Find out if your translation fits the original text. Do not read comments and interpretations of other authors yet; it is the last thing to be done. If you read them first, they will prevent you from having a vision of your own. First, do a grammatical study of the text. It's the basics. What matters is that you know for yourself what the text says. Find out without interference from other researchers, then check by reading what others said.

The revelation of the meaning of the text

Analyze the words in the text individually. Notice how the author used them elsewhere, or other authors in different fragments of the Bible. Original language concordances are helpful, but good grammar can give a clear idea of the correct meaning of the word in question. A good dictionary also clarifies; as said before, it illuminates what the original text says. Textual analysis helps you understand the text as close as possible to the author's original intent.

Study the grammar of the list of words you used in your sermon outline: essential verbs, nouns (names), adjectives, and any grammar facts that matter to you. Find the theological meaning of each word of the text that interests you. Compare the results with your scheme. If you need to amend it, do it.

Enrich the base material of your sermon. Do not put everything new you find in the speech. Maybe it's better to leave it as it can be the raw material for other sermons or series. So keep it where you can find it when you need it. Expository preaching is born from the text, nourished, and lives in the text. It is the Word speaking to the audience.

> In the expository sermon, the preacher does not preach from the Bible but shows it to the audience. God speaks to listeners from it. The correct explanation of the text enriches the theme. Preach the Bible.

Exegesis is likely to give you material for other topics or series. That doesn't indicate that what you did is wrong, but the lighter the points of view grow, the better the audience's understanding. The Word of God is infinite. As a preacher, you can grow with her to intellectual dimensions you don't even suspect.

The rest of the explanation will provide the argument for the sermon. There is no one part more important than another. Each step of the biblical exploration plays a vital role in preparing the topic and the preacher.

It is like clock gear. Synchrony allows God, his Word, the sermon, the preacher, and the audience to collaborate on a common goal: to lead the congregation to Christ. Well, this is the true and primary purpose of the Christian preacher. You can be a good teacher, preach powerful sermons, and be nice to people like you. But if you don't lead the audience to Christ to help them, you have not achieved the objective: save from sin.

Historical-geographical context

Investigate the medium in which the author and recipient treated the text. Human beings are children of an era. Each time generates philosophical concepts and interpretations of life, social customs, human needs, and all kinds of distinctions. It studies the social environment, religious and spiritual context, political influence, surrounding geography, and geographical location of the author and his addressee. Find out how these issues influenced human behavior in their time and how the character or people involved in the text confronted them.

No time is the same as another. Human beings are born in a time, live in it, and receive influenced by it because we are children of the time in which we live. Therefore, you must pay attention to the historical context in which the events occurred or the history that the servants of God wrote. Without Christ, you won't achieve your primary goal: save them from sin.

Sometimes, the events occurred at a different time than when the author recorded them. Pay attention to these details. It is essential to know.

For this, it is necessary to consult serious dictionaries of the Bible, a Jewish encyclopedia, archaeological commentaries on the Bible, and history books of biblical times. Don't worry; almost everything I suggest in this book appears online. You get it with little money. The important thing is that when you speak, you are sure of what you say.

At least two misinformed preachers expressed data out of time in the sermon. One of the stories is true; the other seems like a joke. The first preacher excitedly recounted how young Daniel was thrown into the lions' den. The problem is that the Bible says Daniel was a young man when he was captive in Babylon. He served Nebuchadnezzar until the fall of his empire and survived. It was then that the Persians put him in a government position. He was no longer young. He was an older man.

The other case is an emotional preacher who said in his sermon, "The disciples took the plane from Nazareth and landed in Jerusalem." Then one person congregation exclaimed, "There did not exist planes at that time." But the preacher said, "Well, what was Pontius Pilot doing there?"

Make your conclusions. The more you know about the time the people related to your chosen text lived, the better your textual understanding will be. Understanding this is essential for you to develop an excellent textual exegesis. That is the basis of what your sermon will be. Do not forget.

How did the audience understand it

This is the moment to know what others think of the text. Very few people cheat on you when you have the correct linguistic, geographical, historical, cultural, social, religious, and theological opinions. It will be difficult for wrong points of view to drag you into saying what is not, because you already know what is correct. It is the right moment to read biblical commentaries and consult the idea of different interpreters. Take into account the theological background of the commentator. Be selective.

Discard what you think is inappropriate. Analyze the results critically. Remember, you are not a sponge. You have your concepts that you seek to clarify. If you make a mistake, change them. Have an open mind to change. You want to learn the right thing, and you must achieve it. Never sustain the unsustainable. You can be sincere in your relationship with the Scriptures.

Use the biblical texts in the strict sense. Please don't make the author say what he didn't say. Remember, the textual application has two ways: explicit and implicit. As you know, the explicit "expresses clearly and determinedly one thing"; what is implicit "is included in something else without it expressing it" (RAE). So, to implicit, you can read it between the lines, but you must learn to do it.

You can make an extended application of the text. It is possible, even legitimate, but do not say that this was the author's meaning and that this is how the first readers understood it.

> Bible verses and teachings are helpful in any age. The Bible contains the will of God for man in time.

The divine message does not expire; it has no expiration date. Each verse will remain in effect until Christ comes. As Juan Donoso Cortés said years ago when he spoke of the Bible,

"Book, finally, gentlemen, what when the heavens fold in on themselves like a gigantic fan, and when the earth faints, the sun gathers its light, and the stars go out. He will remain alone with God because it is his eternal Word resounding eternally in the heights" (Miguel de Cervantes Virtual Library, 2018).

The root of the biblical sermon is in the original context; from there, the applications of the evangelical preacher start. What God said to Abraham, he said to him and not to you or your listeners. Your mission as a preacher is to determine what message God brings to your audience from what he said to the Father of faith. That is the current message of the text. Your goal is to figure it out and present it to your audience.

Current text message

The final step of your investigation is to find the actuality of the text message. When you understand what God said to others, you understand what he says to us from the text. You know what you needed to know. Then it is time to apply the result of the explanation to the creation of your sermon or to do an eisegesis.

Exegesis means "explanation and interpretation" (RAE). Eisegesis is when you "say what you want the text to say." So please don't do it; don't invent fanciful meanings. Don't be subjective. Be objective with your audience, and they will thank you. Be honest with yourself.

Enrich your understanding of the Word. Nurture your interpretation capacity. Refine the outline you created and reinforce its content with additional firsthand information. Run away from assumptions. Become a reference for those who want to learn about the things of God. Paul told Timothy, "Preach the word" (2 Timothy 4:2). Practice Pauline's advice.

> Let the Bible speak to listeners on its own. Guide listeners to Christ with the Bible, which is the divine compass. Personal presuppositions are opinions that we all have, but the congregation wants to hear a thus saith the Lord.

Paul also said, "And to the rest, I say, not the Lord" (1 Corinthians 7:12). It was his individual opinion, and he said it. It was sincere. You have the right to have a unique position; we all have it, but let us know if it suits you.

Although I prefer not to preach about particular approaches, the controversy should be far from the preacher. A word out of place can damage your sermon. Think before you talk. People trust the seriousness of the pulpit. Honor that trust. You are clear from which text you will preach. You made a sketch. You enriched it with textual analysis; you got good content. You are close to the goal: your sermon. But it is not all.

This chapter, step 2, is not informative. It only mentions the essential points you must practice if you want to preach with power. Don't read it just to read it. Put it into practice. List the points explained and work on them until you understand their meaning. It is a practice that turns theory into reality. That's why this book promotes practice over theory; try that above knowledge you manage to become an exegete.

Perhaps you have material for several sermons, even a new series. You related what you learned in the explanation and identified each text part, but it is not enough. You may have brought into existence a work of art, but there is a question: Will you expose it to the public from the sketch you created? You still need to prepare the material obtained in your studio for the exhibition.

STEP 3

DOCUMENT RETOUCH

The exposition of your sermon requires that you retouch and simplify the material you obtained throughout the creative process as much as possible. The third step leads to preaching with power. It would help if you polished what you created. Smooth out the hardest. Extract as much as possible from the outline. It is time to subtract. The most challenging thing for a preacher is to get rid of the ideas and phrases he created. Although they are superfluous, sometimes anyway, they seem essential to him.

It would help if you had an excerpt from the outline. Conciseness enables you to memorize the content. It is time to print literary beauty to the sketch. Take away what is left over and add what is missing. It is the arrangement of the content that leads to the form. The way you will say it to the audience.

> Only God is perfect. Human beings need perfection and polish the work we do.

The perfection of our character as preachers depends on our allowing Christ to model us—a work that he performs in us when we allow him to—but that will end when he comes and takes us with him.

First, we can improve our service to God and the task that he entrusted to us. Then your work also can shine.

You and your sermon are pearls in the rough that need to shine. Gemstones sparkle when the jeweler polishes them. Your ideas may be rude jewels, but they need you to smooth them out as best you can. Make them shine like diamonds.

Polishing the sermon is the most difficult; it is more arduous than you have created. Until now, your job has been to accumulate information. But polishing is getting rid of an essential part of the collected material. You've put together material that you thought was great; now, you love it and want to share it with your listeners. Your intention is good, but you must understand that only a tiny part of what you found can fit in a sermon.

It sounds harsh, but it is necessary if you want to preach with power. Learn to distinguish between sand and gold. Observe the material that jumps out among the rest. The precious metal shines with its light. So are the truths hidden in the text. They shine when you isolate them from the rest. The detail makes the difference. Perhaps you think that the important thing is to memorize the data learned during the study. Still, three simple steps can make a difference: imagination, perfection, and simplicity.

Develop the imagination

Do not think that what you need is memory. Einstein said, "Memory is the intelligence of fools " (Muyhistoria, 2018); he believed that "imagination is more important than knowledge." It would help if you had the imagination to turn your sermon into a sparkling diamond.

> To polish a sermon is to take away what is left over. It is leaving a precise amount of information and organizing it ingeniously. Then when others see it, they notice the difference and wonder: this so simple was there?

To imagine is to try to see what you have not seen before or perhaps no one has ever seen. Do not imitate others. Find your vision of things. Find what you are looking for and even what you don't even imagine exists.

Many people study the Bible and think they know it all. Others feel that others already went ahead and said what had to be said. They do not believe that there are still pearls hidden in it.

Solomon said, "By the Lord's mercy, we are not consumed, for His mercies never fail. They are new every morning; great is your faithfulness" (Lamentations 3:22–23). Trust that everything that comes from God he renewed every day. The Bible, which is his word, transmits the divine will. If you believe it, you will look for God in it and find it.

The divine presence next to the human servant is the union that guarantees the preacher's confidence. Do not hesitate. Go to God with humility and simplicity, and allow him to speak to you in the clarity of his Word. Get away from the routine.

To achieve this, do not fall into the extravagance or the complexity of things. Instead, separate the gold from the sand and polish it. Simplicity is what makes the sermon shine; complexity stuns most people. Imagination helps you polish the sketch. Keep in mind that smoothing is removing what is left over. Do it, and you will succeed in this company.

Refine the product

When you have to preach, it seems that the preacher's most challenging task is to find what to say, but it is not. If you worked hard enough, you have a lot to tell. The hardest thing is to give up a good part of the arguments you found.

> Removing content is the hardest thing you will face. We are paternalistic with what we write. It will seem to you that giving it up is a crime.

Sometimes, giving up a sentence is like losing a loved one. Still, even so, it removes the excess information in the sermon. Purify the content. Do not regret removing what is left over. If you do not have material left over, it is that you did not do a good job. It is rare to find a solitaire diamond lying on the clean floor without someone else seeing it before you do.

The gems of your sermon lie jumbled among the information you've extracted. Your job is to find and polish them. It's a time-consuming task that requires the skills you gain when practicing the advice in this book. First, clean the text of what does not weigh enough. Leaf litter prevents others from seeing the genuine product hidden under the dust and straw. It would help if you had the whole grain without thematic contamination.

Lack of weight does not mean it is wrong. Simply, it does not fit in the theme you chose, but with another argument, it can be the best. Please don't throw away what's left over; put it aside for another time. Polish what you need. Maybe it's three promises, two sins, three blessings, or some exciting characters for how bad or good they were. The keyword points to the gems you need. It is the flashlight that makes the gold that you find shine before your amazed eyes. When

I finish my work, I am surprised, and I kneel and thank God who enlightens me. Without him, nothing is possible.

Remember that the keyword is the center of the sermon, and the argument revolves around it. Polishing is a post-production job; you do it at the end. So the whole idea of the sermon revolves around that magic word: the keyword. If these are promises, don't stop until said offers are apparent. Everyone must see them clearly in the shortest possible time.

If they allow you to speak for forty minutes, the time will seem short to explain the three promises announced. The greeting and introduction may take five minutes. You'll spend another ten on each of the promises and have five minutes left to summarize, call listeners to acceptance, and wrap up your message. They will want to hear from you. It seems simple, but it is difficult for you to achieve it without effort.

Cultivate simplicity

The tendency is to believe that greatness arises from complicated things, but it is not valid. The most extraordinary thing is well-organized simplicity. There are many ways to polish the sermon. The three sections of this one need you to purge them of the words left over. "Don't force the reader to read too many words. They will thank you." This is the advice of experienced writers. The same thing happens with speech.

> Don't use twenty words if you can use ten. Start with the title. Prune what is left over. The tricky thing is that you find what does not fit your theme. Please find it and eliminate it without mercy.

When you have what you need, the most important thing is to create a good title. Get people hooked when they listen to it. Short titles are better. Look for the central idea and trim unnecessary connectors like a, of, the, and others. Example: *How to achieve God's promises under challenging times.* Only eight words. It doesn't sound bad, but it can be improved. Perhaps this is more suggestive: *Eternal promises within your reach.* The listener will know the size of his difficulties and will value the offer.

You are not even required to include the keyword in the title. Maybe this would be better: *You can still have it.* It creates more suspense. It is more suggestive and captivates the listener's curiosity. Five words! It has no connectors. There are a thousand possibilities. Be creative. The originality makes the difference. The title is not the sermon; it is the name of your discourse. Up to five words are enough. The shortest titles say more and are better remembered.

I knew a relative who had three names that were not so short. When he managed to say the last name, sometimes, there was no one to listen to him; but today, people don't use so many words. Everything is simplified.

Don't be a minimalist either. A preacher titled his sermons with a word: stick, stone, loaves, fish, etc. A single word almost always says little or defines nothing.

The introduction has three parts: greeting, presentation of the topic, and transitional sentence. The better is a simple, friendly greeting. Next, synthesize the opening and, if possible, summarize the sermon's goal in a concise paragraph, leaving the details for the body. Finally, the transitional sentence is a short phrase whose center is the keyword.

Example: John presented some *promises* we all need to obtain to be happy in our current Christian life. Prune it as much as you can.

Enough: I will talk about some *promises* desired by all. Or any other synthesis. Imagine. Create sentences. Who said those promises, why, and for what? You will explain it later. It's the subject of the body of the message; get to it as fast as you can. Time is running out.

Synthesize the divisions of the body. Build short sentences around the topic indicated by the keyword, in this case, *promises.* It is enough: the commitment to give us a heavenly abode, the guarantee that Jesus will return, and the promise to take us with Jesus (John 14:1–3). Synthesize the main points as much as possible.

> You don't have to include the keyword in every division of the sermon; it's repetitive. Unnecessary.

You said you would talk about *promises.* They know. Jesus prepares a new home; he will come again and take us with him. It could be: They won't forget them.

Sometimes, it is possible to extract the divisions in a single word. In this case, you can exploit the verb conjugation in the infinitive. Example: Jesus promised to give away, return, and transfer; it's the three divisions. Remember, I mean the outline; you explain the details to the listeners. If possible, look for words that begin with the same letter or that their first letter forms an acrostic with the others you write on a blackboard and remember when they go home. They are resources that help the listener memorize the teachings and contribute to learning.

Find an example of this method in my book, *Almost Lost.* It contains eight chapters about Luke 15. Six sessions are about the prodigal son. Many of the subtitles have a word that can work alone. Each word begins with the same letter.

The best sermons stand the test of time as you prune or graft details every time you touch them.

> A good sermon is like a son. You try to improve it whenever you can.

When you grow old and no longer preach, your sermons will have reached perfection. Then you post them.

STEP 4

PERSONAL DOCUMENTATION

Until this chapter, you have come a long way and are about to start preaching with power, but it is still not enough. There is something you need to improve; however, as much as the best, you will need to perfect while you live. That's you. The fourth step you must take to preach with power and improve yourself is personal documentation, which is vital.

You can create the best sermon in the world, but it will depend on your preparation that you impress the listeners.

Your documentation is essential. A preacher is a modern man; he knows about God and understands the times in which he and his peers live. But to preach with power, you need two securities. The first is in God, and the second is in yourself. You have security in Christ. You have the conviction that God called you. You feel the vocation God gave you. Prayer joins you to the throne of grace, and you read the Bible passionately and meditate on eternal things. Do not doubt that God is by your side. Your attitude led you to Christ. He received you, but you also need aptitude.

You trust in what God can accomplish with you, but you must do your part to grow with symmetry. You need to specialize in different areas. The suitability of the instrument can make a difference. Attitude and aptitude must work together so that you can give God the best of you. The first speaks of your disposition, the second of your capacity, of the preparation to fulfill the proposed objective; it means qualities, ability, and suitability.

Preacher training

The biblical expositor is a multifaceted instrument. You put yourself in God's hands, and the Holy Spirit gives you gifts. You learned that biblical ability falls into three categories: capability of doing, speaking, and knowing. Curiously, the exposition of the Word requires all three areas of skills recorded in the book of *Acts of the Apostles.* Preaching is one of the ecclesiastical offices that demands the most preparation.

> The gifts are related to talents—the natural abilities humans are born with and live a lifetime.

You were born with skills that you can use for good or bad. That's up to you. That's why they're talents. You were born with them; they are yours. Your abilities become gifts when you put them at the service of God (Valenzuela, 2005). That is your decision.

God takes control of your life if you put your talents into Christ's service. His Holy Spirit enlightens and strengthens you. It teaches you in many ways but illuminates you to the extent that you collaborate with your instruction—the greater the preparation, the more efficient interpreting the revealed Word. Prophetic revelation connects the servant with the unknown, but enlightenment and divinity benefit the student to the extent of his education. The light increases in proportion to the formation of the disciple.

The Holy Spirit has two missions with the followers of Christ: to teach and to remind (John 14:26), but he enlightens everyone equally. The light of God shines in his Word for all human beings. Although many do not notice it, individual understanding depends on personal preparation and level of knowledge. Your job is to help them see that light from above and lead the sinner to Jesus.

The Bible is within reach of every human being. The Spirit guides them to it, but each one sees the light that emanates from the holy book as far as their tools allow. Jesus did not promise to replace the understanding of his followers but to guide them to the light and remind them of what they studied.

The human part can make a difference in your preaching. The preacher needs the development of the gifts that God gave him. It requires knowledge and wisdom, but it is easier to acquire knowledge than to be wise. Wisdom comes from God. James said to take advantage of the biblical promise, "Ask God for learning, and he will give it to you" (James 1:5).

Knowledge can be elementary or profound. It can grow without limits, but wisdom produces a higher level of experience associated with prudence and the depth to a higher level of understanding (RAE, 2017). Intelligence comes from God; if you have it, develop it.

Socrates had a student who wanted to be as wise as he was. The would-be sage importuned the philosopher to give him knowledge, to the point that the thinker did not find what to do with the impertinent. One day, the genius said to the student,

"Let's go to the sea."

"What are we going to do in the sea?"

"I will give you the first lesson in wisdom."

They walked for a while and reached the beach. Socrates went down into the water, entered a certain depth, and said to the student, "Come closer." The disciple did not associate knowledge with the sea but obeyed. He entered the water and walked to where the wise man was waiting.

The teacher grabbed him by the head, plunged him into the water, and held him tight. The apprentice struggled and kicked until the master's hands gave way, and he emerged to the surface, blowing air and water around him. He was exhausted. He was panting hard. His body trembled while her heart slowed and returned to normal. Then Socrates asked him,

"What did you want most when you were underwater?"

"Air, master, air, air."

"When you desire wisdom as you yearned for air, you will be wise."

Many people are not willing to pay the price of wisdom. Most people study because they want a higher job or think they will have a higher salary one day. When they reach the goal, they stop learning; they settle for limited knowledge. Those who think about money sacrifice the minimum to obtain the benefits they seek. They sacrifice as few resources as possible for personal preparation.

Learning is not a business. A successful preacher craves wisdom like the oxygen or the air we breathe. So if you don't know, cry out to God until He gives you insight (James 1:5).

Santiago says that there is another wisdom: one that does not come from God but from the devil (James 3:15). The knowledge that came from God bears fruit and transmits security (James 3:17). That is the wisdom to which we preachers of the Gospel aspire.

> The faithful preacher goes beyond a particular course of study. It is a willful devourer of knowledge.

He observes the environment in which he lives. As a relentless student, he reads with a critical mind until he understands and identifies the linguistic terms that stand out in the reading information. He perceives the structure of what he reads and uses the content studied. But he never settles.

He is an eternal nonconformist. He wants more because he understands that his work demands more and more of him. Listeners request fresh food daily, but you can only give them part of what you receive. The truth is, "Those who do not study will soon find themselves scraping at the bottom of an empty cauldron." The previous sentence is an old warning to preachers who settle for what they learned in school.

When students graduate from college that day, they may be at least four years behind in their careers because textbooks arrive at university centers after a long writing period. In addition, scholarly editions, printing production, territorial distribution, and storage take about four years. As a result, a college graduate can be an outdated professional.

Professionals update their knowledge through the scientific press, specialized magazines, new books arriving at bookstores, participation in seminars and symposiums, and even radio and television newscasts. Continuing education is an essential tool for companies that respect themselves.

The office of a preacher is no different. Personal growth never ends. It is not mandatory, but it is a requirement for success.

> If you aspire to be a relevant preacher, you must cultivate a solid spirit of self-improvement.

The Bible says, "Examine everything; hold fast what is good" (1 Thessalonians 5:21). The preacher's brain filters the material it receives and separates the bad from the good. As a result, you become a critical researcher. You don't have to know everything, but you should try to understand your vocation as much as possible, and the people around you will benefit from it.

The successful preacher lives in the real world. He knows the people around him. He accepts the virtues and defects of other human beings. He does not pretend that sinners go up to where he is, but he descends and puts himself at their level. He offers pasture for sheep and giraffes simultaneously, but he gives each his own—to each according to his height or level. As a result, all who listen to him feel fed.

Preaching to a diverse audience is hard, but remember, when preparing your message, your responsibility is to feed as many as possible. A misplaced sermon speaks to neglecting the people you purport to help. Be timely. As the saying goes, "Precise, concise, and solid." The speed with which we live requires these three things: accuracy, brevity, and consistency. Rambling leads to mediocrity and absolute failure.

Preacher plateaus

In geography, a plateau is a plain on top of a mountain. It arose from the sea, driven by enormous internal tectonic forces, or the energy of the wind and rain eroded the mountains and created them. They exist hundreds of meters above sea level. They are daughters of the power of nature, but to the preacher, it is different.

The plateaus of the preacher are produced by inaction and conformism; the absence of power creates them. They appear at any height. They happen to good preachers. They happen to those who believe they have arrived, those who get tired, and those who settle for minimal results. For many preachers, they are not plateaus but plains at ground level. They never knew the top of the mountain. They are plains created by the paralysis of growth. The llano is comfortable, sometimes even relaxing. The mountains sometimes tire even looking at them. Not everyone is fit to scale heights.

> Preacher plateaus are states of personal stagnation. They occur when the routine controls the speaker's modus operandi.

In that circumstance, the preacher becomes a predictive entity because people know what they will say in advance. It has no fresh food. His growth has died. So go up the mountain if you want to preach with power. Sacrifice yourself, even if you think you can't. Renew yourself every day. Revive. Go up like eagles (Isaiah 40:31); rejuvenate yourself like the eagle (Psalm 103:5). Work day and night. Train yourself. Don't stop growing. When you get stuck, take strength, look up to the sky, and continue your ascent to the top because she is next to Christ. You are more than a climber. Next to Jesus, there is no fear.

Plus, it would help if you had courage. Climbers use ropes to hold on, picks to dig up slopes, hooks to hold on to rocks, special shoes to prevent slipping, shockproof suits, and many other accessories. But above all, they develop will and courage. All those tools without the aptitude lead nowhere. You also have tools that help you grow. Get them and use them on your way to the top but have Christian will and courage.

Proper spiritual tools can prevent a plateau from emerging in your career. Instead of making the journey uncomfortable, the preacher's plateaus disgust people. Still, to the preacher, they serve to rest and continue the ascent toward the summit. Relaxing can be the end of power as a communicator of God. God doesn't get tired.

Preacher's tools

Preacher training requires some special tools. First, you need general and particular knowledge. Then it begins with what you need most: training and personal preparation. The experience arises from the sum of the specific effort. You apply it to each topic you develop. Unless you enter a ministerial college, the best path to travel for you is to become self-taught.

Not everyone travels the same path to reach the pinnacle of their career. Theory and practice advance together. The method arises from the opportunity. The idea is born in a traditional or self-taught way, but if the average student does not try more than what the teacher demands, he may not get far. Sometimes, interest produces better results than opportunity.

Many achievers did not attend college, and thousands of college students failed. Success results from purpose coupled with perseverance. You can achieve what you set out to do. If you don't have another chance, study for yourself. Document yourself as much as you can.

The Bible is the source that nourishes the preacher. Still, his tools are Bible commentaries, Bible dictionaries, Bible concordances, and any literature that adds knowledge.

The tools exist in physical and electronic forms. Electronic media fall into two main categories. First, study programs and then tools of work. This chapter includes essential aspects of electronic media in preaching as tools for preachers. Because learning to use them will save time in organizing the materials.

Bible concordances

Several biblical concordances exist. Many preachers use a concordance Bible because it seems to them that this is the best and almost only tool. She relates preachers to some essential verses, but their contribution to biblical research is limited. A good concordance is the *Complete Bible Concordance*, by William H. Sloan, which contains a comprehensive organization of the Bible in verse-by-word alphabetical order. Now the electronic programs are more efficient; when the student searches, the verses appear instantly. The important thing is that you quickly find the verse you are interested in consulting.

There are two basic ways to use a concordance: to find a verse quickly or to create thematic lists of verses. With it, you locate a text or verse thematically and gather similar or related verses. Concordances speed up the work of gathering the necessary verses.

The best option is to purchase a concordance that meets your needs. Today, you can find them on the Internet. The *New Strong Exhaustive Concordance* is available at reasonable prices, depending on the seller. There are others, but a good one is enough. You may find some for free in electronic *PDF* format. There are "free" and paid electronic concordances on the net. In the end, nothing is free. Decide the price you want to spend on the supplier.

> The point is that you get a valuable tool for your work as a preacher. Do not pretend to do an excellent job if you do not have the necessary knowledge and tools.

From my laptop, I do almost any research; but that is a topic that we will see later. The following section presents a good Bible dictionary as one of the main tools of a preacher.

Biblical dictionaries

Bible dictionaries are one of the preacher's most essential tools. You can find them in many sizes and depths. Get the most respected ones; no need to run after a bunch of dictionaries. Sometimes, a good one is enough.

Dictionaries hardly comment on matters that create controversy. Instead, its function is to show the meaning and origin of words, verbal roots, data about certain characters, the historical background of countries, ancient cities, territories rich in events of biblical interest, wars that have taken place, and endless social incidents related to biblical times.

Bible dictionaries help clarify the origin of words and their meanings. In addition, if you're looking for nouns, they also contribute timely historical data, social customs, cultural issues, religious differences, and more. But it all depends on the preacher and the topic he is looking. Nevertheless, they are handy tools for investigating biblical matters, for some, the most necessary.

An easy one to get is *Vine: Expository Dictionary of Old and New Testament Words*, which appears online in electronic form. But if you search, you will find other options.

Use the dictionary as the first tool of your study. It helps you interpret and define the central aspects of the sermon outline. Please choose the one you like or collect some of them. Then compare the results with each other.

Bible commentaries

When my father accepted the Gospel, he wanted to interpret the Bible correctly. So he asked the pastor of the church how to do it, and he told him that there were biblical commentaries that helped to interpret the sacred text. So he traveled to Havana and visited Modern Poetry, the best bookstore in the country. He asked for a Bible commentary.

The manager asked,

—What religion do you want him from?

—What does religion have to do with it?

—Man, each religion has its own thing.

—Well, if that's the case, I don't want any. I need a book that explains the Bible without religious interpretations.

—I am sorry.

The bookseller left him at the counter, and he quit having a Bible commentary.

The Bible commentaries are one of the main tools of the preacher, but there are many types of them. Many people have commented on the Bible and published personal ideas, well founded or not; that's why you have to be selective.

The commentary, like dictionaries, conveys historical, geographic, social, and cultural information; dates of events; word meanings; and other data—but all this, together with the interpretive concepts of the author. As for the first, they are pretty exact. In the second, it depends on the line of thought of the interpreter.

When we were studying Juan's writings, a teacher said in class that more than four thousand commentaries have been written on Juan alone. Just from John! Each author interprets to the best of his ability or according to the light he received.

There are amateur and professional commentators. You may have a hard time defining whether a comment is authoritative or not. Each of these books represents the opinion of the author or authors who wrote it. Comments have two main lines of documentation: informational and interpretive.

Some time ago, someone told a story that seemed unusual. He narrated the story of a famous writer who was writing the history of the world. That writer spent most of the time at his desk, near a window from the upper floor where he was, allowing him to look out at the street from time to time.

One day, while he was writing, he heard how the neighbors crowded in front of the building and talked and shouted louder and louder. Finally, the shouting reached such a magnitude that he couldn't take it anymore. He placed the sheets of paper on one side of the desk and looked out the window. Two men were fighting each other. He watched as one stabbed the other to death. The writer's servant, who had seen the fight in the street, went up the stairs to tell his master what had just happened.

He ran into the room and said to his employer,

—They killed John.

—I saw it from the window.

Surely, he saw how John attacked Peter, and Peter killed him in self-defense.

—I didn't see that; Peter killed John for no reason.

—No, sir, that was not so. I was there.

—I saw it from this window too.

As they disagreed, they went down the street to check with other witnesses of the event, and the neighbors gave reason to the servant. The writer, crestfallen, went up the stairs. He went to the desk, took the stack of sheets of paper he had written, and went down to the street.

He called the servant, and in the presence of the neighbors, he said,

—If I cannot correctly interpret what I have just seen with my eyes, I cannot write the history of the world without having seen anything.

—Sir, what are you going to do with that book?

—Burn it down.

— Have you gone crazy?

—No, but I am an honest man.

In the presence of all, he burned his life's work.

Be careful when researching doctrinal matters. The interpretation of facts is where the differences lie. That is why it is good that you consult the most accepted commentators in the Christian world. The above is one of the reasons why it is not suitable for you to read comments from others before you build your sermon outline. It's easy to get sidetracked from your original thought if you don't have a solid interpretive foundation.

An excellent biblical commentator is not dogmatic. The interpreter or interpreters say or expose the different positions of the exact text. They say, "We believe this, but there is this and that interpretation." The student perceives when the researcher is sincere in what he says.

> One of a sincere researcher's virtues is accepting that he does not know everything. So leave room for others to comment. Even when you believe your conviction, you respect the right of others to dissent.

A sincere researcher is critical. Being critical is not the same as looking for other people's flaws. Being critical is learning to discriminate respectfully between what we believe and what others think. The preacher's goal is not to judge a particular comment but to understand and document his sermon. So focus on the data you need to know.

You go to the biblical commentary, search for what you need, examine the opinion of other authors, and confirm the integrity of the search. Of course, the fundamental objective is not to include everything others have said about the topic you chose in the sermon.

But you corroborate that you are not wrong in your approaches and perhaps use some data that seem relevant to your point of view.

Electronic media

Today, the most practical thing is to learn to handle electronic media. The existing variety is excellent. When I say electronic media, I mean hardware and software. You can have the most extensive library you have ever imagined on a computer. You can take it with you wherever you go. With little money and a few clicks, you can have different versions of the Bible, Bible commentaries, Bible dictionaries, Bible concordances, and hundreds of books at your fingertips. Then, as you write your outline, you use all that material with another few clicks. You save a lot of time.

The computer

Years ago, I wrote sermons with a pen on sheets of white paper, sometimes yellowish, because I had no other options. But despite living in Cuba, I aspired to have something better. One day, while walking down the street, I saw a man on the porch of his house selling a typewriter. The apparatus was of solid cast iron, branded Remington. He had a skeletal appearance and weighed a lot of pounds. It didn't have the "Ñ" or accents because the keyboard was English. The man told me, "She doesn't speak Spanish, but she can adapt. There are mechanics who adapt the Ñ and the accent. Here, they invent everything."

From the looks of that artifact, it was perhaps one of the first writing machines built. Possible that it had many years of use. In Cuba, people lived in the past and believed it was modernity. So I didn't realize that perhaps that artifact was a valuable antique. Since I wanted to progress and stop handwriting, I bought it for thirty Cuban pesos after a brief haggle—a small sum that in Cuba was a lot of money. It was more difficult for me to take it home and learn how to use it than acquire it. I used it for several years, but the desire to improve led me to the computer.

Maybe you think you don't know how to operate a computer. Don't grieve. The first time I saw a computer was in 1995. I lived in Cuba and promoted missionary work in the administrative office. I wrote a draft by hand and gave it to a secretary to type. There were three or four obsolete typewriters in the office. But they were for the secretaries; no one else was allowed to use them, not even to write a sermon. It was not easy to be authorized to use them for another purpose. They were revered gadgets. In Cuba, any fret is a treasure. They were revered objects in full use.

But that year, a Christian organization in the United States donated a computer for the secretaries. It was a 386 desktop PC. So finally, there was a computer that the five or six secretaries would use during the eight hours of work.

One morning, I saw the new machine on the desk of the president's secretary. Employees surrounded her as if a UFO had landed there. No one dared to connect it to electricity. It was necessary to wait for a technician to arrive that the president had hired to teach how to use it. It was an unproductive day at the office. No one was concentrating on work.

During the day, we discussed no other matter. People abandoned any responsibility to observe the inert device that the United States replaced with a new one and transferred to Cuba for them to use. But many believed they were ahead of the latest invention available.

Two days later, the technician arrived. He worked for the government, the only one with access to electronic media in the country.

In ten minutes, he assembled the parts, connected a small printer with the PC, and plugged in the cables for electricity, and there was light. The first images appeared on the screen, and Word loaded. Then the technician started the first lesson.

We didn't fit in the small office, but someone leaned into the room and said, "Classes are for secretaries." So I left the premises before they expelled me.

I called the technician and told him I wanted to learn computers. My idea was to pay him for the classes, but he told me, "Computers are nonsense; this equipment and programs are designed for you to learn on your own. So stay near. I will finish them and show you how to handle them and where to find the word help. In this, success equals a ton of hours sitting in front of the computer. After that, it's just practice."

They removed the old typewriters from the office a few days later. And the secretaries were taking turns doing their homework on the PC. Work was almost at a standstill. Then, finally, I understood that one cannot depend on what is foreign and that these means are personal.

I traveled to the United States and got my first computer in those days. A new machine. I bought it in pieces and managed to get Cuban customs to authorize its entry into Cuba. Then I paid a technician to put it together. It was a desktop PC 486 DX4. With her, I began my experience with electronic media. Since then, I have had various computers.

Get a computer, even if it's second-hand. Today, it is an indispensable tool for the preacher. But unfortunately, most of the study centers do not accept handwritten works. It would help if you learned to use a word processor. There are several, but the most popular is Word.

If you can acquire a new team, congratulations. Otherwise, don't worry; second-hand can also give you good results. The important thing is that you advance your purpose of being a successful preacher.

Don't fall behind brands. Buy the one that is within your reach and that meets your needs. Don't invest too much if you are not going to produce money. Nowadays, the average modernity time of electronic equipment is from six to eighteen months. They are quickly obsolete. Soon they would bring out better ones than yours. But don't worry. This is a market issue. What matters is that any equipment fulfills its functions for many years.

> Do not enter the competition, or it will ruin you, and you will not be happy. But use what is within your reach.

The best computer for a preacher is a laptop. The preacher is a traveling worker. Sometimes, he is in one place, and other times he goes to another. Imagine that you can move with your team and a library of hundreds of copies of electronic books, which you use wherever you go, without moving to another site. You work in airports, on airplanes in midair, on public transportation, in the hotels you stay in, in churches you attend, and more.

Nowadays, almost every place has a place to connect a laptop. The point is to start somewhere. Start and learn alone. When in doubt, if you don't have anyone to ask, ask Google or YouTube.

The digital programs

Bible research has many digital programs within reach. These contain Bible commentaries, Bible dictionaries, Bible concordances, and Bible versions in different languages. There are also free and paid ones. One of the most popular is *Logos Bible Software*, which contains a complete library. It's not free. But there are other free ones.

One of the most common programs is *My e-Sword Bible*; it's free. You can have it on your computer, on a tablet, and even on your phone. Also, you can change it to your preferred language. *My e-Sword* has a collection of bibles, commentaries, and dictionaries. It is practical, saves time, and contains good information. In addition, this program has a section called "downloads" where you will find books and bibles of all kinds. You can download a good part of these for free; you have to buy the rest. It was not expensive. Remember, it is good that you invest in your training.

You can also find the *2011 Adventist Christian Library*. It contains a Bible commentary, a dictionary, and the *1960 Reina-Valera Bible*—more of a spiritual library. The important thing is to get and master the work tools. Then you will learn to handle them.

You learn to use them by using them. Investigate for yourself; it will initially seem impossible, but you will see progress over time. There are slight differences from one program to another. Still, you will discover that they work similarly: the commands change shape and place but perform similar tasks in the end. The first thing you should do when you get a new program is to seek help. The help shows the researcher how to handle the program; the rest is practice.

Before using it, try to understand how it works. Activate the different commands you find and discover how they work and what you get from them. Get a general idea of how it works. It is easy. Don't work until you know how to use it and what each command does. It's like driving a new car.

When you buy a new car, or this is new in your hands, unless you want to have an accident, you don't jump in and shoot out onto public roads. First, you read the manufacturer's manual, and before leaving, you test drive the vehicle as best you can.

When I was a child, I heard the story of a man from the village who wanted to ride a motorcycle. He dreamed of riding one, but he was poor and couldn't have it. Then one day at a baseball game, he saw a friend on a motorcycle. The game was in the field, in a paddock, and he said to his friend,

—Let me take a ride on your motorcycle.

—Do you know how to drive a motorcycle?

—It's like riding a bike; I ride a bike.

The friend lent him the motorcycle. The man grabbed the machine by the handlebars, wheeled it over to the baseball infield, and kicked the starter lever down. The machine worked. Then he crossed his leg over the seat, sat up as best he could, grabbed the cranks, put the gears in with his right foot, turned the crank, and took off. The viewers never knew at what speed it ran.

He started spinning around the baseball infield. At first, people ignored it, but as it accelerated, the driver widened the circle and rotated around the baseball field diamond. Every turn he made brought him closer to the fence, a barbed-wire barrier stapled to a live hedge of bushes. The viewers expected the worst.

Some laughed, while others shouted, "Stop, stop, stop!" But the motorcyclist could not find the brake. He called, "Find a rope, throw me a lasso, tie me up, throw me a lasso, stop this! I'll kill myself!" Despite the mobilization, they did not arrive on time. The handlebar brushed against the fence, and the pilot fell to the ground, wallowing in the motorcycle.

There are two extremes: those who think they know it all and those who believe they will never learn. Think that everything is possible but that you must learn. The Bible says, "All things are possible to him who believes" (Mark 9:23); "Without faith, it is impossible to please God" (Hebrews 11:6).

> Life is progress. Don't settle for who you are. Look far and go by faith.

You can complete your preaching kit with an electronic tablet if you're computer savvy and learn some research programs.

Electronic tablets

There are many types of electronic tablets on the market. The most popular is the iPad. It is expensive, but different models exist. Many use them as a toy, while others use them to read electronic books. But the use of tablets is broader.

Tablets also have a word processing program: Pages, Word, and others. It depends on the brand. You can have an electronic library, write your sermons, save them in folders by categories, and preach them from the tablet. They are an essential tool for the preacher. They eliminate the paper.

Sometimes listeners get distracted, wanting to know how many sheets of paper are still left before the sermon is over and the preacher ends the exposition. They lose the sermon by counting sheets of paper.

With the tablet, you replace paper with electronic documents; you eliminate stationery from the pulpit and the desk or file. The paper gets lost or fades, and time turns it yellow and brittle. After a time, they are not functional. Sometimes, they confuse the preacher.

Sermons on paper are difficult to modify. You end up scratching out paragraphs, scribbling on paper, and writing them all over again. Sometimes, they ask you for a sermon, and you don't have it at hand. You don't even remember where you saved it. It isn't easy to carry a briefcase full of books and papers. Keeping papers has become a tedious and unproductive job.

You can write your outlines in the tablet's word processor. Then, you access the library, study the Bible, investigate the biblical commentaries, consult the dictionaries, look up verses in the concordances and copy the citations you need. You do not require a computer. There are even keyboards that you can attach to the tablet, which work like a laptop. What you need is practice.

Success is in the organization. You buy books and save them in Play Books, Amazon Kindle, or e-books. There are others, but these are among the most popular because Amazon, Google, and iTunes contain three of the world's leading bookstores. Choose the ones you consider necessary. Digital books are on the rise.

A paper book is still a good option, but there are reasons for you to buy electronic books. You get e-books instantly with one click, they're much cheaper, they don't take up shelf space, and you can take them with you wherever you go. In addition, there are millions of electronic documents in *PDF* and other formats on the net that you can get and save on a tablet.

Also, you can create folders and save the books and materials by subject. Hundreds of books have free or paid download apps on Google, Play Books, and the Apple Store: bibles, Bible commentaries, dictionaries, and whatever literature you need.

Success lies in the level of organization that you apply to the different programs and documents. Like all things that succeed, your ability to put an order in your actions is the basis of success. You can even have many of these advantages on your phone.

You can also enjoy team synchronization. For example, if you have an iPad, a Google tablet, and a smartphone, you can read the same book from any of your devices.

You get the book on Kindle, Play Books, or others, start reading them, close them, and switch activities. At another time, you open another of your computers, in the same place or another, find the book you were reading on the previous device, and open it. The new computer asks, "Do you want to continue reading where you left off, or do you want to start on a different page? New page?" You tell it that you want to continue reading, and it takes you to the page you last read on the previous computer.

A tablet is a formidable tool for the preacher. You organize your library, read and underline books, prepare and save your sermons, and preach them from the tablet without printing them on paper.

Although if you want to print them because you are addicted to paper or want to give a copy away, you can pass them to the printer with a couple of clicks. You don't need a cable to print if the printer is good. And it's not the only thing you can do with a tablet. With the tablet, you take pictures, edit them if you have an image editor, and save them in it. You also record the sermons and edit them if you have an audio editor.

There are professional audio recording programs available for three or four dollars. You can record with the computer's microphone, although it works best with a Bluetooth or lavalier microphone. They are cheap and record with enough quality. The rest is editing. But where to save data when you run out of space on your computer?

The clouds

Today, there are electronic clouds. Currently, yes, some live in the clouds. It is real. It's no longer offensive to tell you. It is an Internet computer system that works on remote servers which manage information services and applications. Some clouds are OneDrive, iCloud, Dropbox, and others. Companies in charge of digital information manage clouds. The digital sky is cloudy all the time. There are clouds of all sizes and prices.

Consumers use these applications, called clouds, and store the information outside the devices. They acquire storage capacity at a low cost. Most companies allow free access to a permanent quota of between five and nine gigabytes. If you want to use more, you have to buy space. However, the monthly fee is cheap. The cloud has advantages and disadvantages.

Advantages: You can store a large volume of information off your hard drive. You can access that information from any computer and any geographic location with an Internet connection. If your equipment is damaged or stolen, you do not lose the data. Your material has protection against catastrophes and carelessness. With a phone, you can access your sermons anywhere there is a signal. You are always ready to preach. It seems like a lie.

Disadvantages: You store your information on a foreign server. If you cannot connect to the network, you have no way to access the information. On the other hand, cyber hackers can steal or damage data. If they are sermons, they are good even when stolen from you; perhaps the thieves will convert and steal no more. So you lose the speeches, but you gain a soul for Christ. It was worth it.

If you don't like clouds, buy high-capacity hard drives. They have dropped in price. The new solid-state drives are more secure and three times faster than the old ones. However, I advise you not to put all your eggs in one basket. Hard drives are fragile. It is better that you replicate the information on different devices. It's a matter of choice, but better to be safe than sorry.

Those who can buy a house to their liking do not rent it. But those with a lot of money sometimes prefer to rent. Sometimes, you make decisions because it is the way you solve your problem. It is good to know different ways to do the things we need. They are ideas; take them as you see fit.

These are some of the preacher's tools—perhaps the most important. It depends on the taste and the possibilities of each one. Once we acquire the tools, what remains is the search for information.

Information search

The word information, like any other, is abstract. Alone doesn't say much. It depends on the sense you use. Research works when you know what you are looking for and how to achieve it. To look for something, you have to know it. If you don't know it, it's difficult to find it.

A cleaning manager complained that an employee did not pick up all the garbage when he was cleaning. "He's young, has good eyesight, and leaves the garbage because he wants to. It damages the company," he said.

"I don't think so. He's a good person. Probably his concept of garbage is not the same as yours. Teach him what garbage is," I said.

"You were right," he said later.

Einstein said some interesting phrases about the mind: "The mind is like a parachute. It only works if we have it open." "We are all very ignorant. What happens is that we are not all ignorant of the same things." "All science is nothing more than a refinement of everyday thought." "The important thing is not to stop asking questions." "Imagination is more important than knowledge." And "creativity is intelligence having fun" (www.muyhistoria.es/articulo/quincefrases-de, 2018).

Searching for data requires imagination. Develop intuitive thinking.

Creativity is the essential quality of the human brain, according to Einstein. He said that "creativity is the fruit of emotional intelligence."

Your brain can be a professional tape recorder, recording thousands of gigabytes of information per minute, archiving it for a lifetime, and reproducing it exactly when needed. Still, you won't create much worthwhile stuff if you can only do that. To investigate is to imagine something and try to find it. You make it when you turn your imagination into reality.

Bibliographic research

Bibliographic consultation is when you examine what other authors have said about your topic. Please do not get a series of citations. Cut them out of their matrix and paste them into the matter. You may need to know the authors' opinions; don't confuse them with the explanation you did. The task is to document the sermon.

You documented the sermon when you did the explanation and added the details related to the base biblical text. The documentation tries to resolve the questions that surround the text. Situate the sermon in a natural, credible, cultural, religious, and historical setting. It is the explanation you made of the text. This other information is secondary; you need to update what you researched. Nothing more.

Copyright rules

With the Internet's widespread presence, content use has become simple. You can enter the network and take what interests you. It's simple. Almost any topic appears on the net. You write a few words and are already on track with what you need. Unless you know how to use it, it's not a good idea.

Sometimes people like the easy way. Apart from the fact that it can be a crime, this does not favor your personal development. To show what belongs to others as one's own is dishonest and a crime. The creation of another person never tastes the same as your own, and you must memorize even the most insignificant data you find.

You don't have to memorize your creation. Just say it because it's yours, and you dominate it. It's your daughter. You know her well. Someone else's product is the one that costs effort to make it look like its own. It is difficult to learn concepts from others, and it can be tedious. Beware of plagiarism.

> Listeners notice when you imitate someone. For example, a saying goes, "It is better that you be a bad you than a good other."

But above all this, using other people's materials can become plagiarism, and plagiarism is a crime.

One day, a senior pastor visited the church of one of his junior pastors. In the church dressing room, the leader told the older man the Bible reading they would read and the hymns the congregation should sing. The young pastor said,

—Pastor, what topic will you talk about today?

—Don't worry. You'll soon find out.

The elder organized the worship procession, reviewed responsibilities with the participants, and directed the music director to go into the temple and perform the music for the public appearance of the pastoral entourage. As they walked toward the front door of the altar, the host pastor said to his boss,

—Pastor, what topic will you talk about today?

—Don't worry. You'll find out soon enough.

The cult seemed normal. An old man got up from his chair and read, "And the Lord said: I will wipe out from the face of the earth the men whom I have created, from man to beast, and even creeping things and the birds of the sky; Well, I regret having done them" (Genesis 6:7). They prayed on their knees and sat down.

Next to the leader was the host pastor. His nerves wouldn't let him sit still. He touched the chief on the shoulder and asked,

—Are you going to preach the flood sermon you preached at the meeting?

—Yes, what's wrong with it?

—When you preached it, I copied it and preached it here a week ago.

—No. Boy. It can't be that. How can you do something like that? Let's see how I fix this now.

—I'm sorry, Pastor. I didn't know this was going to happen.

—God helps me; pray for me.

After the opening hymn to the sermon, the president stood behind the pulpit, greeted the congregation, opened the Bible, and said,

—Last week, your pastor preached to you Deluge I. Today, I will preach Deluge II.

And it's true; copycats rarely get it right.

There are legal and honest ways to do well. For example, if you copied the sermon, tell the listeners. Mention the author's name, and people will applaud your honesty. When you quote another author, credit the quote, enclose it in quotation marks, and say where you found it. That will save you from making a fool and becoming a dishonest preacher. Use other people's ideas, but give credit to the author.

You copy the biblical texts in quotation marks, and at the end, you write the chapter and the verse in parentheses. Do the same with author citations; enclose the phrase, sentence, or text in quotation marks, and at the end, have the author's name, the book's title, the year of publication, and the citation page in parentheses. When you quote more than two or three words from another author, you must put them in quotation marks. Verify the citation. If you paraphrase another author, you must credit the source. Make it basic.

In universities, complicated manuals record multiple styles and dozens of rules to cite an author correctly. Even computer programs can determine if your research contains plagiarism, a mistake you can make unintentionally. Plagiarism is another factor you should avoid; that is why you should use the Bible alone when creating the basis for your sermon. The other is originality, a matter related to the previous one.

Data inclusion

A sermon is not a string of data linked by the author. Speeches are in the Bible. They live in it, and you have to find them. They are there in front of you. You outline a biblical text, discover a sermon, make the outline, and then document it. It's that simple when you put the correct method into practice. Exegesis is answering the questions of the text and looking for what others have said about it. You already know how to cite other authors, but be moderate when including other people's thoughts. Be yourself.

Sermon content

The information is not the content of your sermon but the topic you outlined in the textual investigation. Documentation provides the foliage that makes your point of view believable. You can't say much in a sermon, so you must master the art of creating a series of topics. Sequences are good because they allow you to distribute arguments over time. You organize the information, ration it, and distribute it in the series. That's why you learned to sketch.

The sketch is the backbone, the skeleton that structures your future sermon. The meat, the skin, and everything else you put it, standing behind the pulpit, in the presence of the audience. That is why preaching is an art. The audience is an eyewitness to a good part of the construction of the sermon. Listeners witness how you turn the skeleton into a living body. So please bring it to life, dress it up, and even decorate it unless you take a written sermon and read it.

The speeches read are formal literary pieces for specific occasions. The sermon is something else; it conveys a life that rarely emerges from reading a pamphlet. Sure, if you can't preach a sermon, at least read the booklet you wrote, but as long as you depend on reading, you will not be a powerful preacher. No one bound can walk without inspiring pity.

You manage to preach with power when your intellectual baggage grows, and you put yourself in the hands of God. Then you are released from bondage, the Spirit controls your mind, and words flow freely. You create from a simple sketch.

The preacher's baggage

After hours of study, you may think, "I have wasted my time, I worked so hard, and I used a minimum part of the material obtained in the sermon." If that happens to you, be happy. You will succeed. Remember, "for the preacher to have confidence in himself, his preaching must represent ten percent of what he knows about the subject."

You can't measure how much you know. Still, it's a way of saying that if you want to speak with power, your knowledge of the subject must outnumber the arguments you present in the sermon. It is the preacher's way of cultivating trust in God and himself.

The preacher must know where to get the additional arguments he needs. If someone asks more about the topic, you should be able to answer with authority. Also, if you forget an opinion, you should be able to substitute another one.

The Spirit often leads the preacher down a different path than he had planned. It is the divine will's way of teaching you beyond the private chamber where you prayed to God for wisdom, studied the Bible, pondered what you learned, and prepared your outline.

You can preach a series ten times in different places. If you record the sermons, you check that you did not repeat the same argument in each area where you preached. The brain refuses to repeat arguments as it registers them; it seeks variety.

Repetition is an act preconceived by the author, imposed by circumstances, or self-imposed to achieve a specific goal. You can't spend your life memorizing every word of your sermon. Even the audience unconsciously pushes you to create new forms from the same points of view.

Remember Einstein's phrases: "Imagination is more important than knowledge," and "creativity is intelligence having fun." So you need to be creative and develop your style and arguments.

> Don't be sad or feel less if you can't create in public. What matters is that you try. Practice makes habit.

Repetition conditions reflexes. Perhaps one of the primary brain functions is automation. Think about how many tasks you perform automatically, without thinking about them. Sometimes you believe that patience and procrastination will help you achieve it. It is not like this. If you want to preach with power, preach until you make it. The essential thing is practice.

A journalist asked a skater boy,

—How did you manage to skate so well?

—Getting up every time I fell.

When I was a child, I wanted to ride a bike. I wouldn't have believed it was possible if I hadn't seen so many people moving suspended between two wheels lined up one behind the other.

I got on the bike, and a friend held the back of the vehicle and tried to balance it, so I didn't fall on the dam full of potholes overflowing with water. He pushed me without letting go and with a terrified panic that I would fail. Others had fallen and had scrapes on their knees and arms. He did not progress in learning.

One day, a cousin appeared. He was a tall and muscular young man. He told me,

—Upstairs, get on the bike.

I went up and felt how he grabbed the bike and started running down the embankment. Then, as he increased the speed, I shouted,

—Careful, careful, slow down! You're going to knock me down.

He paid no attention; he gave the vehicle the highest speed. As a result, the bike lost the weight that used to knock me down. Either he did it right, or he fell to the ground. Without thinking, I controlled the handlebars while turning the pedals with my feet. It seemed to me that I was floating on the dam while avoiding potholes full of water and mud. Then, a fleeting thought struck me: "I almost dare to drive alone."

By the time we got to the end of the ride, he was out of breath. Snorted. With a broken voice, he said,

—You know what? Most of the time, you drove alone.

—I do not think so. It's just not possible. I don't know how to ride a bike.

—During the last stretch, I ran to catch up with you.

—I thought if I had known earlier, I would have ended up on the floor.

After that, the rest was easy. It's the method I use to teach others to ride a bike. For example, I recently taught a granddaughter how to pedal without falling. In a few minutes, she was alone on her bike. She was surprised. I hadn't done it before (it's not a formula for you to repeat and break someone's bone. In my experience, everyone is responsible for their actions).

The preacher's baggage has continual use. It is a lifesaver in difficult times. It guarantees poise and control in the face of circumstances. The luggage is the source of help that nurtures creativity. God enlightens him to find what he knows.

What happens to the preacher is enlightenment. The Holy Spirit fulfills the promise of Jesus and reminds you of what you have studied. God enlightens your knowledge so that your brain delights in creating. But the size of your flashlight matters.

> The preacher's lantern is his preparation. The more you prepare, the better the Holy Spirit enlightens you. He shines on things revealed so that you can see details you've never seen before.

Revelation goes beyond illumination. It is when the prophet receives visions and dreams about matters that he does not know. Sometimes, you have not even heard that they exist. Sometimes, we confuse inspiration with lighting. As a result, you are unlikely to improvise. Instead, the Holy Spirit enlightens you. The words flow from your mouth like the water of a waterfall when it slips between stones. It runs downstream toward the riverbed that takes it to the sea.

What you know today as improvisation probably isn't. The preacher improvises the discursive forms when he brings up part of the content stored in his intellectual baggage. It is difficult to devise the unknown.

In the unknown, revelation replaces illumination. The preacher transmits the voice of God. It is not improvisation but communication of another's message, in this case from God. It is a prophetic inspiration. But most preachers are not prophets.

Many who do not preach well believe that they lack technique, but what they do not have is something to say. Increase your intellectual baggage, and you will see the results. When you are filled up, you will exhale it even through your pores. Fill yourself with Christ and his Word, and you will speak with power. You will have plenty of things to say to people. But of course, you will have to dose what you say or lack time.

Content dosage

A saying goes, "It is as bad to go as it is not to arrive." It is terrible to know little, but accumulating too much knowledge on a subject can be fatal. No matter how great your intellectual baggage is, the content of what you say is important. It is no good throwing an avalanche of information at the audience that buries them in their seats. As said before, most people don't take in more than two or three ideas at once. They don't remember them.

There are two basic ways to bore the public: the talk of the inconsequential and the profusion of knowledge. The chatter and rambling in the content tire the listener and make him run away. The excess of knowledge overwhelms the intellect of the audience. No matter how serious you say, people don't learn what you've internalized over years of study in a few minutes. They need time to assimilate what you say.

> The preacher who does not study inspires pity. The one who tries to teach too much at once produces rejection. They accuse the first of being a fool and the second of being conceited. But both run the same risk: failure.

We once heard a preacher go on longer than he should have. Suddenly, a listener said to the one next to him, "Let's go; this man talks his head off." Public speaking requires restraint. An old piece of advice says, "End the sermon at its best. They should want to listen to you again, not run away because you bore them." Another saying goes, "A sermon does not have to be eternal to be unforgettable."

You dose the content when you administer what you know. They like your preaching. They would likely ask you to preach to them again. If you nurture them every time you feed them, they will want you to come back again and again. When you preach to the same congregation many times, they grow, and so do you.

As you share your baggage, you need to increase it. The growth becomes reciprocal; you look for them to receive, and you receive when you share with others. If you say too much at once, they won't call you back. You will get stuck. You will have plenty of time, but the knowledge—they won't call you to share it.

The illustrations

Illustrations are another essential aspect of preaching. A teacher said, "Illustrations are like the windows of a house; they let in light." The illustrations, apart from illustrating, change the scenes and prevent boredom. The cinema has specialized in the art of scenography.

Movies, reports, soap operas, and any cinematographic product project a varied and changing scenario. Before, they said that the scenes could last up to three minutes. Today, the characters interact more quickly. Today's life is faster. It requires more movement.

The preacher should not spend more than three minutes at any point in the sermon. Long explanations give the impression of being stuck, and listeners wait for the topic to progress. The progression provides movement to the speech, but the illustrations facilitate a break in the thematic progress. They help to reflect and fix the lessons in the viewers' minds. There are many kinds of examples.

Biblical illustrations

The biblical illustrations are good, probably the best. The Bible is full of valuable facts and characters to corroborate your arguments. In it, there are illustrations for all the subjects you preach. It does not matter that they are not new. What matters is the approach. You can adapt them according to the theme.

The listener is often surprised when he discovers that there is another vision of something that he thought he knew well. The faithful preacher understands that no one has said everything about something. He knows that each point has many edges and searches for the hidden ones until he finds them.

We live in a three-dimensional world; the Bible has many dimensions and points of view because it comes from God, who is infinite. Look for the correlation between different biblical themes. The Bible is a whole, a unique book, and each subject is interwoven with the others. Illustrate your sermon with biblical examples.

Personal illustrations

Personal illustrations are some of the best. What happened to you is firsthand. It is your experience. Each person has their own story. Almost everyone has something interesting to tell; the secret lies in how to say it. The specialty of cinema is to turn irrelevant into the center of attention of others.

A painting attracts more than a photo. Anyone with a phone takes a picture, but not everyone paints a picture. The photo contains every detail of the image. It is routine; not even those who take these photos look at them again. On the other hand, a painter paints what he considers essential on the canvas, and the blurring dissolves the rest into the background. Photography becomes art when the photographer imitates the painter and emphasizes the central over the secondary, achieving that effect when the lens blurs and the scene fades. It achieves this when it highlights the significance and hides the irrelevant.

Good illustrations do not include the whole story. Instead, the speaker extracts the parts that interest the sermon's content and limits the story. It is just an illustration; telling it all takes time and can take the focus off the topic.

Personal illustration has two primary dangers: diverting attention to the preacher and a distasteful approach to listeners. Suppose you put too much emphasis on what happened to you and go on longer than necessary. Then, the listener can lose the thread of the sermon; the latter occurs when the preacher sets himself up as a role model.

The audience is amused if you tell them that you were cheated, ripped off, and even nearly beaten to death. Listeners are welcome when you tell them how you overcame a test, how God answered a prayer, and many other stories. But don't tell them that you are the holiest person in the world. Don't set yourself up as an example of spirituality. It does not look good.

The only model to imitate is Christ. Paul said, "Be imitators of me, as I imitate Christ" (1 Corinthians 11:1). You are not Paul. Modesty is better than pedantry.

Real-life illustrations

There are also real-life illustrations. Again, Jesus used the examples of the medium in which he preached. A description is not a pretty story. As ridiculous as it may seem, it is a mention that clarifies what you said. Jesus illustrated his message with the seed, the plants, the lilies, the birds, the fish, the yeast, the net, and dozens of figures known to his listeners. They were small strokes distributed with wisdom in what he explained.

To illustrate is to lead the listener from the known to the unknown. Real-life is full of examples. We would pay any price for a picture book during the seminar. They are not bad, but sometimes, they lead the listener out of their social environment toward cultures the audience does not understand. What for you is real life; for another, it can mean the most absurd nonsense. Even words can change their meaning in another latitude.

When I left my country, I realized I was saying words that offended people from other latitudes. So I had to internalize a series of changes. They were words that appeared in the dictionary, but in other places, they had obscene, denigrating, or lousy taste meanings. In one of my first sermons outside my country, a person caught my attention, and it wasn't because I said an obscene word.

I preached about the prodigal son. The Bible says, "He wanted to fill his belly with the carob beans that the pigs ate" (Luke 15:16). In my country, they call the food of the pigs "sancocho." In Cuba, even atheists have a riddle that says, "Which is the dirtiest saint?" And the answer is "San cocho."

In Cuba, the sancocho can be a smelly mixture of human food waste or the food that pigs eat. So at one point in the sermon, I asked, "Would you eat sancocho?"

I noticed that some would have eaten it, and others even wanted it. Their mouths were watering, as the saying goes. They were courteous to me. I changed the affair and continued with the sermon.

As I was leaving, a lady told me, "Pastor, I want you to know that in my country, sancocho is a delicious dish. It is a well-seasoned broth with meat, many viands, and other things. It's exquisite."

"In my country, that is called ajiaco. I like it a lot," I said. She was satisfied, but I still don't say sancocho to ajiaco or mention it when I preach.

Real-life illustrations must have specific characteristics. The audience must understand what the preacher is referring to—they do not create confusion, they do not evoke obscenities, they do not offend anyone, and they clarify aspects of the sermon. The words must be precise even if none is the same as another because the synonyms are close to the meaning but do not say the same thing. For example, many people agree that pretty is distinct from beautiful. Beautiful is not necessarily pretty. Both words are synonyms, but they express different aspects.

> Don't get illustrations out of the listeners' context. They won't understand them. People don't even understand a joke out of context. Don't use worn illustrations. The worn doesn't help. It hinders.

Sometimes, I heard the same illustrations from different preachers. Students who left the same school repeated them in the various places they went. They did not realize that other colleagues had passed before them and had said them. The worst was when someone said it happened to him. Listeners called him a liar. Don't say it happened to you if it didn't. If they discover you, they will stop trusting you. You run the risk of being told. If you don't have a suitable illustration, look it up or make it up. But be original.

The plausible in the illustration

The plausible is credible. You do not know if it has happened, but you mention it as if it were an actual event. Jesus used even the unlikely; the parable of the rich man and Lazarus is one such illustration. Jesus used a widespread belief to illustrate a truth: after death, there is nothing you can do to change your destiny.

Jesus told parables like two sons sent to the vineyard (Matthew 21:28–32), the wicked farmers (Matthew 21:33–46), the wedding party with an identical dress for the attendees (Matthew 22:1–14), the ten virgins (Matthew 25:1–13), and the parable of the talents (Matthew 25:14–30). The ministry of Jesus was full of accurate or plausible comparisons, but Jesus is the Teacher of teachers. Do not abuse creativity. You are not Christ.

If you tell a plausible story, try to make it truly believable. Create a worthwhile image. Let it not be a story. The unbelievable, vulgarity, and lies are in bad taste in preaching. The preacher stands out for his ability to lead the flock to good pastures and fresh waters (Psalms 23). But unfortunately, so much ingenuity can be adverse to the preacher.

Negative illustrations

Negative illustrations lack spiritual meaning. Trivia is in bad taste. They may teach truths and lessons, but they don't fit in the pulpit. Sinners want to know how to improve their lives. Your sermon should lead them to Christ and guarantee a genuine encounter with him. Tales and fables do not help much in this task.

The tales

People don't go to church to hear ghost tales and descriptions of animals behaving like human beings. We all like stories. The phrase remains, "Tell me a story, Grandpa."

Fantasy predominates in tales. Although there are more fanciful than others, as stories, they exist to entertain more than to teach. The preaching is neither a tale nor aims to amuse the listeners. When someone is not serious, they call him "tell tales," which is not a good connotation for a preacher. There are different varieties of stories, but their style is not for preachers. There are satirical and scathing tales within the story, but they are inappropriate for illustrating sermons.

The fables

Fables are more serious than tales; they wisely show the behavior of human beings. They put the behavior of real people into the mouths of irrational animals. They alert us to the danger of human attitudes. They help us suspect that risk can arise behind certain too-good or bad forms. Fables are popular wisdom expressed humorously. They are not suitable for preaching.

Listeners prefer that you tell them the truth as it is. Because evil exists and is there in front of everyone, it is not about a little animal that acts this way. Evil results from a natural enemy that lies in wait like a roaring lion to devour you (1 Peter 5:8). Warn them of this danger so that they take care of themselves.

The funny in preaching

The humor in preaching can be beneficial. A proverb says, "Laugh and the world will laugh with you; cry and you will cry alone." But the preacher is not a clown who works to make people laugh. The mission is not to make people laugh but to lead them to Christ. The humor in preaching does not arise from a joke but from how things are shown. Wit can be funny; sometimes it makes you laugh. But it is not learned; it is a gift with which one is born.

It arises in the natural way that people speak. Making people laugh is a rare gift. It is easier to produce tears. Some are specialists in making others cry. They even delight in doing it. It is enough to offend a sensitive person, and tears immediately flow. Laughter and crying come out of emotional states, but it is easier to cry than to provoke laughter.

Some people are experts in manipulating emotions, but preaching should not be manipulative. Neither to make you laugh nor to provoke tears. The secret to the success of the preacher is to move the emotions and the intellect of the listeners at the same time. It's not about making them cry or laugh but about getting them to make the right decisions. Let them follow Jesus.

The joke in preaching

The definition of "joke" is "a sharp and funny saying or occurrence. Drawing with humorous, caricature or critical intent, with or without text, generally referring to current affairs. Funny and festive event. Chanza, mockery, joke" (RAE, 2017). The quotation contains four primary meanings.

Being funny is not telling stories. The joke is more profound than the story. Observe the four meanings given by the RAE, and you will realize what is useful and what is not in preaching:

Saying or sharp and funny occurrence

drawing, caricature, or criticism, referring to the current topic

funny occurrence

chanza, mockery, joke

Of the four meanings, only one can be helpful to the preacher—the first: "a cute and funny occurrence." The difficulty is that this way of speaking almost always arises from the natural vocation of the speaker. It is neither learned nor it is studied in schools or in books.

That is why it isn't easy to make people laugh in preaching. Those with this gift do not go out of their way to make people laugh or plan it. People laugh because they notice how naturally they express the truths they say. Listeners accept hard facts laughing.

Preaching is not a caricature or a funny occurrence, and even less a joke or mockery. The sermon is not about entertaining, making fun of someone, or teasing people. Instead, the preacher seeks to lead people to Jesus so that he may transform and save them.

Laughter in preaching

Most likely, Jesus's preaching made people laugh. Jesus was profound and intelligent in his way of saying things and provoked immediate reactions. He peculiarly taught the people the analysis of his way of speaking and acting hints at the behavior of those who listened to him.

For example, "pass a camel through the eye of a needle" (Matthew 19:24). Don't worry about which eye of the needle Jesus referred to. It is a debatable fact. There is more than one opinion about it: that it is a sewing needle or a small door in the big door of the wall. Never mind, either case is of unlimited occurrence.

Jesus spoke of an impossible. Do not try to make it possible to show that Jesus was not wrong. Instead, he gave an unbelievable example: passing a camel through the eye of a needle.

Imagine someone threading a needle with a camel between his fingers. Sometimes, it isn't easy to put a thread through the eye of the needle. Imagine doing it with a camel. It was a funny, comic statement.

Then the idea arose that perhaps Jesus was referring to a small door in the great gate of the wall. Those who remained outside after the guards closed the main entrance entered the city. That small door was called "the needle eye." It was for a person to enter on foot. There are reasons to think that Jesus did not refer to this door.

The first reason is that it seems that these doors were invented about a hundred years after Christ. The second reason is that Jesus illustrated an impossible. When someone with a camel was left outside the city, with much effort, he entered through the needle's eye. With great effort, he dismounted the load from the camel, kneeled the animal, dragged it, and brought it in before the presence of some who mocked and others who pitied or perhaps did not care. It wasn't easy, but it entered. Jesus illustrated that a rich man could not enter the kingdom of heaven unless God transformed him.

But no matter what eye of the needle Jesus was referring to, think about the emotions of those who heard Jesus. Either interpretation must have made them laugh. What do you think people did when they saw someone dragging an empty camel through such a small hole? How did they react to imagining a person threading a needle with a camel? They probably laughed.

Another case occurred when the Pharisees asked Jesus if they should pay tribute to Caesar. People expected a complicated answer, perhaps like the one given by the Pharisees and the Rabbis. Some were doctors of the law, but Jesus only asked one question: "Whose image is this, and the inscription?" (Matthew 22:20). To their astonishment, he said, "Give to Caesar what is Caesar's, and to God what is God's " (Matthew 22:21). What do you think the people did when Jesus's accusers fled in terror? They probably laughed.

That is why they killed Jesus because he ridiculed human wisdom. They hated Christ because he made fools of people who were proud of their knowledge. They thought they were wise, and Jesus humiliated them in public. As a result, people perceived at a glance that the truth was in Jesus. That is why he said, "I am the way, and the truth, and the life; no one comes to the Father except through me" (John 14:6). He showed them that outside of him, there is no salvation possible.

> The fun of Jesus's preaching was not in telling stories, telling fables, or entertaining people; the grace arose from the wisdom in his words.

Contrasting the complicated teachings of the rabbis with the simplicity of Jesus's words, he amazed the people and made them laugh. Everyone was amazed at him. The enemies of Jesus said, "Never has any man spoke like this man!" (John 7:46).

No man will ever speak like Jesus. He is the Teacher. But go ahead and do the best you can. Don't try to be funny if you don't have the gift. People laugh at naturalness and criticize those who pretend. If you have the advantage of making people laugh, you don't have to try to achieve it. The natural is born and grows alone. Cultivate it and use it for the good of the people. Thank God for the gifts he gave you.

Don't plan to make your listeners laugh or cry. Don't play with people's feelings. If they cry or laugh at your sermon, let their emotions spring from the remorse of their hearts touched by the Holy Spirit acting through your spontaneous message.

The wisdom in preaching

To illustrate his preaching, Jesus used naturally pronounced linguistic means. He displayed an unmatched ability with human language. Christ used exaggeration, sarcasm, simile, and parables.

He used human language to express divine will to his listeners. For him, words were the tool he used for his work. From this, it follows that if you need a tool, you do not look for the most complicated but the one that best performs the desired function. Do not invent flourishes, rhetoric, vulgar jargon, and others. Stand up to someone sent by God.

The use of hyperbole

Jesus used exaggeration. He recommended to sinners that they control the members of the body that induce them to sin: "Take out the eye that sees what is not to be seen, if your right-hand acts badly, cut it off" (Matthew 5:29–30), and he exaggerated the importance of one's own sin in comparison with that of his neighbor. He wanted us to know that the fault that loses us is ours and not that of our relatives, friends, or neighbors. He said, "First remove the plank from your eye, and then you will see clearly to remove the speck from your brother's eye" (Matthew 7:3). They are not the only cases. Think of the difference between a blade of grass and a giant beam. It seems exaggerated, but it shows a lesson: your problems should matter more to you than other people's.

Exaggeration as a preacher's tool works like a scientist's microscope. It allows him to show listeners what is invisible to the naked eye, the hard to watch. This resource is called hyperbole. It means

"Excessive increase or decrease of what is being talked about. Exaggeration of a circumstance, story or news" (RAE, 2017). It is a suitable method for people to perceive reality without being offended.

The sarcasm

Sarcasm is another linguistic resource available to the preacher. Jesus also used sarcasm. He warned his disciples that to enter the kingdom of heaven, they must have "a righteousness greater than that of the Pharisees" (Matthew 5:20).

Were the Pharisees righteous? Jesus called justice what was not because he wanted his followers to take their eyes off what everyone believed was the best example of spiritual behavior.

Jesus also called the Pharisees "healthy" because they did not associate with sinners and said, "He has no need of a doctor" (Matthew 9:12). Is there a person who does not need the divine Physician? The statement was condemnation and not praise. It was sarcasm.

Misused sarcasm can be cruel and destructive. The RAE defines the word sarcasm in two ways: an offensive weapon and a literary resource. "Bloody mockery, biting and cruel irony with which someone or something is offended or mistreated. Use of irony or mockery of sarcasm for expressive purposes" (RAE, 2017). So be careful with this resource. You must know how to use it because irony can be cruel.

One teacher said, "You have no right to offend your listeners because no one pays them to listen to you; they do it because they want to." However, sarcasm used carefully and gracefully, with good purpose, is acceptable. Indirectly show people their faults and make them think and look for solutions.

The simile

Another linguistic resource is the simile: "comparison or similarity between two things" (RAE, 2017). It illustrates something by comparing situations or things we detest or admire. Jesus also used the simile.

Jesus invited his disciples to fish for men (Matthew 4:19). He said that the church is "the salt of the earth" (Matthew 5:13) that preserves life and gives flavor. Finally, he compared his followers to a light held high so that it shines for all to see (Matthew 5:14–16). Jesus was the master of the simile; for everything, he had a comparison.

Peter used the analogy to point out the negative, comparing false prophets and lying teachers to "fountains without water" and "stormy clouds" (2 Peter 2:17).

The simile, well used, is a powerful tool. Jesus led the audience from the known to the unknown. He used comparisons related to the daily life of his listeners. It makes no sense to compare with the unknown. If they don't understand you, listeners don't react. Sometimes, they don't even know what you said.

The parables

The parable is a story that contains an important lesson that we want to teach the listeners. Again, use comparison and similarity, but it is more comprehensive. It tells a well-informed story, and the listeners will deduce and extract the moral or spiritual teaching in the report. Jesus spoke in parables. They were his favorite tool to teach his listeners.

Remember that illustrations are complementary, no matter what resource you use to illustrate what you're saying. Remember the windows of the houses. They are neither many nor few; they are the ones necessary for the light to pass through. Have common sense.

Two great genres of preaching

Preaching encompasses two great genres: didactic and evangelistic. Didactic preaching is for church members, while evangelistic is for winning nonconverts. One of the main concerns of the preacher should revolve around the confirmation and growth of the followers of Jesus (2 Timothy 4:1–5).

Paul recommended to Timothy attention to the church and evangelism. Evangelism strengthens the church and attracts outsiders. A good evangelistic campaign builds membership because it consolidates the members in the truths they accepted and attracts and convinces new followers.

> The church is unlikely to grow when there is no balanced preaching in it.

So let us analyze both aspects separately.

Didactic preaching

Didactic preaching builds the Christian life of the believer, nourishes the congregation, strengthens the spiritual foundation of converts, and teaches sound doctrine. The preacher focuses the theme on the spiritual growth of the followers of Jesus. Is formative. It prepares them to withstand the attacks of ravenous beasts, as Paul warned about the church's enemies (Acts 20:28, 29).

If you want to preach sermons that meet the expectations recommended by the Apostle, implement these five recommendations in your preaching: preach to converts, guide the believer, feed the congregation, strengthen the disciple, heal the spiritually sick, and preach sound doctrine.

But they are not simple; didactic preaching covers more than this. But first, it is preaching to teach. Still, these aspects strengthen the concept of what it means to care for the flock of God. I have a purpose statement that has helped me lead the congregation successfully: "A well-fed, healthy, and happy church is a growing church." I have experienced it.

Through it, the preacher addresses an audience converted to God. The first responsibility of a preacher is to feed and care for the flock of God. Second, it guides the believer on the Christian life and provides the congregation. Third, it strengthens the spiritual foundation of the audience and leads them to sound doctrine.

Evangelistic preaching

Evangelistic preaching presents a simple message. It does not clutter the listeners' minds with many complicated biblical passages. Instead, it preaches the need to accept Christ to be saved, promotes the acceptance of Jesus, and invites the unsaved to receive him as Savior.

Evangelization is a separate topic that requires specific characteristics of the speaker and specialized knowledge of the evangelist. But keep in mind some essential attributes of evangelistic sermons.

The evangelical message is Christ-centered because Christ is the center that attracts sinners. The science of evangelism goes beyond teaching listeners theology more than any other message. It includes the element of persuasion.

> As you preach, listeners should feel the Holy Spirit drawing them to the cross of Christ. Therefore, the preacher focuses each point of the sermon on moving the intellect and emotions of the audience.

Serial preaching provides an opportunity to delve into evangelistic content. But don't go off the rails. Instead, trace a progressive path before the audience. The presenter focuses on the steps toward salvation: love of God, redeeming love, the consequences of sin, repentance, conversion, transformation, obedience to God, hope in Jesus, redemption, surrender to Christ, commitment, and others.

You don't have to include them all in the series. Use the most necessary within your evangelizing plan. It depends on the number of topics you intend to present to the audience.

Think of a topic, choose the biblical text, outline the text, prepare the sermon, and try to find the previous steps toward salvation in it. The rest is to work and polish the sketch when you have them. The most challenging thing is determining the focus of the different parts of the text. For the rest, almost any text leads you to the same goal: Christ.

List the steps to salvation and keep them with you. Write the list in the order you consider logical for the sinner to accept. Then present a progressive message, perhaps: divine love, redeeming love, acknowledgment of sin, repentance, confession, obedience, etc. Do not worry about the chosen text. The Bible is full of these messages and repeats them thousands of times. The biblical story is the history and perspective of the human species to the so-called divine redeemer. It narrates the involvement of God, who is love, with rebellious humanity, who barely understands the holy sacrifice to save us.

The human being is the same at any age. Every event where people interact contains elements of doom and salvation. Identify them and apply the list of evangelistic themes. It is your tool until you train and identify them with the naked eye. I have dozens of series that appear different but approach the same steps from different angles. The subject does not change, but the point of view does.

You do not need to mention the theme. It is enough for you to classify the human attitudes found and describe how the different actors proceeded. It would help if you made it look simple. Let them see people act and make decisions for better or worse. Let them imitate the positive actions and give up the negative ones. Let them convert.

Being a preacher makes you a divine instrument for the good of humanity. You do not work for yourself; your employer is God, who calls you, attends to your needs, and sustains you. As great as your talent may seem, it is not you who discovers the truths between stories told thousands of years ago. God, through his Holy Spirit, shows them to you.

Therefore, he does not ask you to discover what exists there since before you were born. Your job is to dust off the hidden treasures, collect them, organize them, store them neatly, and show them off to people. A job that seems simple, but it is not.

If you want to do it, you must prepare carefully. Sacrifice yourself. Study. Invest time and resources in your preparation. Coincidence does not exist; only those who fight succeed. If you want to preach with power, be a steadfast student of the Bible.

You preach with power when you get the Holy Spirit to grab you, speak for you, and move your listeners. You speak with power when you get rid of yourself, and the listeners look at God before them and hear the voice of Jesus whispering in their ear, "Follow me." Sothey follow him, and you disappear in time while they continue with Jesus and live with him for eternity.

If you propose it, you will achieve it. Don't stop in time. Take advantage of this momentum and move towards the goal of your life: to preach with power. Jesus sent you to the lost, the Holy Spirit is there to guide you to them, and the Father wants you to be involved in the redemptive work that envelops the entire universe. Do not give up. Keep it up. You will become the powerful preacher for Christ that you long to be.

REFERENCES

Biblioteca virtual Miguel de Cervantes. (s.f.). Obtenido de Cervantesvirtual: www.cervantesvirtual.com

e-Sword-the Sword of de Lord with and electronic edge. Version 3.0.0. (1 de 1 de 2000-2021). Greek New Testament (Byzantine) w/ Strong´s Numbers). Comentario Strong de Génesis 1:26. (R. Meyers, Ed.) Franklin, TN, United States of America. Recuperado el 27 de junio de 2022

Lockward, A. (31 de 10 de 2018). Bibliatodo. Obtenido de Diccionario-bíblico/homilética: www.bibliatodo.com

Muyhistoria. (20 de 9 de 2018). Quince frases de Einstein. Obtenido de muyhistoria: www.muyhistoria.es

Real Academia Española. (2014). Diccionario de la lengua española (Vigésimo tercera edición 2014 ed.). España.

Valenzuela, A. (2005). Los dones espirituales. Pasadena, CA: Living Ministry.

Vyhmeister, N. W. (2009). Manual de investigación teológica. (E. vida, Ed.) Miami, Florida: Zondervan.

NOTAS

www.ingramcontent.com/pod-product-compliance
Lightning Source LLC
LaVergne TN
LVHW091002080826
845145LV00003B/1089